From Your Friend ... **THE MAILBOX**

OCTOBER

A MONTH OF IDEAS AT YOUR FINGERTIPS!

PRESCHOOL– KINDERGARTEN

WRITTEN BY

Deborah Burleson, Janet Czapla, Jayne Gammons,
Ada Hamrick, Lucia Kemp Henry, Carol McPeeters,
Mackie Rhodes, Sarah Tharpe-Winchell

EDITED BY

Lynn Bemer Coble, Ada Hamrick, Mackie Rhodes,
Jennifer Rudisill, Karen P. Shelton, Gina Sutphin

ILLUSTRATED BY

Jennifer T. Bennett, Cathy Spangler Bruce,
Pam Crane, Teresa Davidson,
Clevell Harris, Lucia Kemp Henry,
Susan Hodnett, Sheila Krill,
Rebecca Saunders,
Barry Slate, Donna K. Teal

COVER DESIGNED BY

Jennifer T. Bennett

TABLE OF CONTENTS

October Calendar 3
Highlight special days in the month of October.

"Classroom News" Newsletter 5
Keep parents up-to-date with this reproducible newsletter.

The Lovely Leaf Season 6
Your little ones will "fall" for these autumn-leaf projects.

Family Ties 16
This unit on family connections is "knot" to be missed!

Fire Safety Is A HOT Topic! 26
These activities will spark youngsters' interest in fire safety.

Simply Spiders 36
Arachnid activities even Little Miss Muffet would love!

Any Way You Slice It 46
Ready for delivery—pleasing pizza ideas for your little ones.

Oodles Of Noodles 49
Explore the "pasta-bilities" with these nifty noodle activities.

Pop…Pop…Popcorn 52
Good with butter or without—
Popcorn's fun; there is no doubt!

Good Night! Sleep Tight! 55
These nighttime ideas are sure to delight!

Meet The Cornfield Crew! 65
Aw, shucks! Little ones will love this "corn-y" collection.

Project PUMPKIN 75
Get your P.I.'s—Pumpkin Investigators—snooping around the
pumpkin patch.

It's Trick-Or-Treat Time! 85
Youngsters will go batty over these ghoulishly good ideas for
Halloween fun!

October Calendar

National Dessert Month

Mmmm! The month of October is the time of year to indulge in your favorite dessert! During group time, invite students to share the names of their favorite desserts as you write them on a sheet of chart paper. Ask youngsters to describe how some of these are made. Then, on separate sheets of white construction paper, have each child illustrate the dessert of his choice. Encourage him to dictate a sentence telling about his picture. Assemble the pages between two construction-paper covers to create a class book titled "Dandy Desserts."

2—Birthday Of Charlie Brown® And Snoopy®

On this date in 1950, the comic strip PEANUTS® by Charles M. Schulz was first published. This cartoon strip is so widely read that it is written in 26 languages and appears in numerous newspapers around the world. Cut out several PEANUTS® strips featuring Charlie Brown® and Snoopy®, and glue them on a sheet of tagboard. Read the comic strips aloud to youngsters. Encourage students to compare the relationship between these two characters to that of real owners and pets.

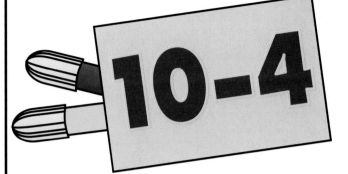

4—Ten-Four Day

Radio operators use the code words "Ten-Four" for "yes." On this day, post a sign printed with the numbers "10-4" in a prominent place. Encourage students to use this special code when giving affirmative replies today.

12—Columbus Day

On this day in 1492, Christopher Columbus reached the shore of the Americas. He referred to the native inhabitants of the land as *Indians*. Believing that the Indians could be easily befriended, Columbus offered them gifts of red caps, strings of beads, and other small tokens. To provide lacing practice, give students a variety of beads and laces. Encourage them to offer their completed projects to friends to wear for the day.

(Turn the page for more…)

14—First Sandwich Made

In England, the Earl of Sandwich invented the first sandwich by placing meat between two slices of bread! Today the ever popular sandwich is served at almost any meal with almost any kind of food on it. For snacktime, have each student make a peanut butter–and–jelly sandwich to commemorate this special invention.

15—National Grouch Day

Do you know any grouches? If so, this day is for them! Throughout the day, be sensitive to youngsters' feelings. If a child appears to be particularly grumpy, offer him a grouch grab bag—a small, paper bag containing stickers, small toys, or soft candy—to cheer him up. At the end of the day, offer all the other students a bag to take home for the next time they feel grouchy.

24—Birthdate Of Sarah Josepha Hale

Known as one of the most famous magazine editors of the 1800s, Sarah Josepha Hale was also credited with convincing President Lincoln to make Thanksgiving a national holiday. In 1830 she wrote a poem called "Mary Had A Little Lamb." Today this poem endures as a popular children's song. For fun, read aloud a storybook version of this rhyme; then have youngsters join you in singing the song.

27—Birthdate Of Theodore Roosevelt

Theodore Roosevelt, the 26th president of the United States, was born on this day in 1858. Because he was a sickly child, Teddy exercised and worked hard to improve his health. He grew into a strong, healthy adult and an avid outdoorsman. The stuffed animal known as the *teddy bear* was named after this great man. Invite students to bring their favorite teddy bears to cuddle during a special reading of *Where's My Teddy?* by Jez Alborough (Candlewick Press).

31—National Magic Day

Magicians across the country take note of this day to observe the anniversary of the death of Harry Houdini, the great magician and illusionist. To commemorate National Magic Day, teach youngsters this simple magic trick. Mix a few drops of dishwashing detergent with a small amount of water. Have each child dip his finger into the mixture, then write his name on a window or small mirror. When the name dries, encourage him to make it reappear by fogging the glass with his breath.

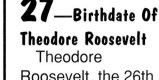

October

CLASSROOM NEWS

Teacher: _____ Date: _____

A Peek At The Week

Looking Ahead

Reminders

Help Wanted

Special Thanks

The Lovely Leaf Season

'Tis the season to study leaves and all of their lovely autumn colors. Your youngsters are sure to fall for the pile of language, literature, math, and art activities included in this multidisciplinary unit. So what are you waiting for? Jump in!

by Lucia Kemp Henry

Let's Go On A Leaf Hunt

Fall days are perfect for brisk walks outdoors with your youngsters. Plan to take your students for a walk on your school grounds, around your school's neighborhood, or to a local park. During the walk, encourage youngsters to collect freshly fallen leaves of different colors and shapes. (Newly fallen leaves have moisture in them and are more suitable for pressing and preserving.) As youngsters collect the leaves, talk about the different attributes—the colors, the shapes, and the sizes—of the leaves. Collect the gathered leaves in a large shopping bag.

When the children are ready for a break, have them lie down on the grass under a tree that is in the process of losing its leaves. Ask your students to watch the leaves falling from the tree. If the wind is blowing, have them close their eyes and listen to the leaves moving in the wind. On your walk back to school, play an autumn version of I Spy. Ask youngsters to look for trees that are mostly green, red, yellow, brown—even purple! It looks and sounds like autumn has arrived!

Pressing Leaves

When you return from your leaf hunt, have your youngsters help you press the collected leaves to prepare them for use in classification activities, counting activities, and art projects. To press the leaves, you will need a supply of newspaper, some heavy books, and several large pieces of cardboard. Place several sheets of newspaper on a piece of cardboard. Arrange a single layer of leaves on the paper; then top with several more sheets of newspaper and another piece of cardboard. Continue layering cardboard, paper, and leaves in this manner until you have prepared the desired number of leaves for pressing. Evenly stack the books on top of the last piece of cardboard. Leave the materials undisturbed for about ten days. Then carefully remove some of the leaves from the layers. Prepare the removed leaves for counting and classification activities by gluing each leaf onto a white, poster-board square. Laminate the poster-board squares. Leave the remainder of the pressed leaves under the paper to be used for art activities at a later time.

Seasonal Sorting

Learning about size, shape, and color is bushels of fun when your learning tools are lovely leaves. For this seasonal sorting activity, use the leaves prepared in "Pressing Leaves" on page 6. Or, after duplicating page 14, prepare the leaf shapes on page 13 for use by laminating the page and cutting out the leaves. Create a classification board by cutting a sheet of black poster board to resemble the shape of a plastic garbage bag. Attach a yarn tie if desired. Label a colored card "Leaves" and attach it near the top of the board. Similarly label additional cards with words that focus on the attributes of size, shape, and color. To the back of each card, attach the loop side of a piece of self-adhesive Velcro®. Attach the hook side of two pieces of self-adhesive Velcro® near the top of the board. To begin the sorting activity, attach two of the size, shape, or color classification cards to the board; then encourage youngsters to sort the leaf cards or leaf cutouts in columns beneath the classification cards.

Big Book Of Leaves

Following your leaf sorting activities, inspire your little ones to collaborate on the creation of a class big book. Stock a painting easel with red and yellow paint. Provide each child with a personalized sheet of art paper and ask him to paint either a big or small leaf using one of the provided colors. When the paintings are dry, bind them between construction-paper covers. Title the book and decorate the front cover appropriately. Ask each child to describe his painted leaf using the color, shape, and size words learned in "Seasonal Sorting." On his paper, write the child's descriptive words to complete a sentence similar to the one shown. Provide each child an opportunity to share his page with the class; then read the book together as a group.

Sam

Sam's leaf is big, red, and pointed.

A Lovely Leaf Song

Reinforce youngsters' abilities to classify autumn leaves by singing this song to the tune of "London Bridge Is Falling Down." Each time the song is repeated, ask a volunteer to suggest a new size, shape, or color word. For visual appeal, have the volunteer also display a leaf card or leaf cutout that corresponds to his chosen word.

See the [red] leaf falling down,
Falling down, falling down.
See the [red] leaf falling down
To the ground.

Red Leaf, Yellow Leaf

Leaf through *Red Leaf, Yellow Leaf* by Lois Ehlert (Harcourt Brace Jovanovich, Publishers) and you'll discover a wonderfully seasonal story that focuses on the growth of a maple tree. As you read the story aloud, encourage youngsters to carefully observe the collage-style illustrations. Challenge them to identify the natural objects—such as the maple leaves, roots, seeds, sprouts, and twigs—that are incorporated into the illustrations.

As a follow-up activity, have your youngsters help you make this fall display that will burst with color. Cut a tree shape from brown bulletin-board paper; then mount it on a background. Using the pattern on page 12, prepare maple-leaf-shaped templates. Ask each child to use a template to trace and cut out several red and yellow bulletin-board-paper leaves. Have him gently crumple his leaves, then slightly flatten them. To each of his leaves, have him tape a brown pipe-cleaner stem. Pin or tape the leaves to the background, arranging them above the tree trunk to form a colorful canopy of fall foliage. If desired, add labels to identify the various parts of the display.

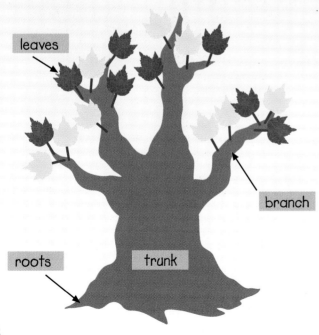

Where's The Leaf?

What could be more fun than a daily treasure hunt? Select one of the large, pressed leaves prepared in "Pressing Leaves" (page 6) to use as the treasure. Brush several coats of Mod Podge® Gloss-Lustré medium onto each side of the leaf, allowing the leaf to dry well between each coat. If desired, sprinkle a small amount of gold glitter on the leaf while the last coat of Mod Podge® is wet.

Each morning before your little ones arrive at school, place or hang the leaf in, on, under, above, or behind something in the classroom. When your youngsters arrive, ask, "Where is the leaf?" Encourage them to describe the hiding place using prepositional phrases. Once youngsters are familiar with this activity and the position words, have each child make a "Where Is The Leaf?" booklet.

"Where Is The Leaf?" Booklet

For each child, duplicate the booklet pages on pages 14–15 onto white construction paper. Have each child create a leaf in the appropriate area on each of her booklet pages. To create the leaves, have each child attach various materials, such as leaf-shaped stickers or stamps; small, real leaves; and leaf-shaped sequins—or use various techniques such as sponge painting, drawing, and stenciling. When each of her booklet pages has a leaf, encourage each child to color the booklet pages and the lid, tablecloth, and child patterns. For each child, cut out the booklet pages and the patterns. Assist each student in gluing the lid pattern to page 1 of the booklet, the tablecloth pattern to page 3 of the booklet, and the child pattern (decorated to look like herself) to page 5 of the booklet. Staple the pages together along the left side.

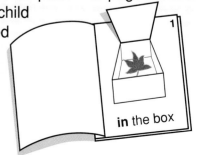

in the box

Leaf Manipulatives

Use more of your pressed leaves (see "Pressing Leaves" on page 6) as manipulatives for these activities. Or, using the leaves on page 13 as patterns, cut leaves from autumn colors of construction paper.

Pattern Cards

Glue leaves or leaf-shaped cutouts to sentence strips to create pattern cards. Encourage youngsters to use the cards and the leaf manipulatives to create and extend patterns.

Sorting Sacks

Fold down the tops of two paper grocery bags. Label one bag "big" and the other bag "small." Challenge youngsters to sort the leaf manipulatives by size.

Tree Counting Boards

Color and cut out ten poster-board tree shapes. Label each tree with a different numeral from one to ten. Direct youngsters to identify the numeral on the tree, then count and display the corresponding number of leaf manipulatives.

Leaf Journals

Your little ones will probably be fascinated by the color and movement of beautiful fall foliage. You may even observe that their simple explanations of the world around them seem almost poetic. To record their thoughts, make these leaf journals for drawing, dictation, or creative-writing activities. Cut a piece of poster board identical in size to a sheet of art paper. Using the leaf pattern on page 12, trace a leaf shape onto the center of the poster board. Then cut out the shape of the leaf from the poster board, being sure to leave a frame around the cut-out shape. Set the cut-out leaf aside. For each child, clip the frame to a sheet of colorful art paper. Have each child paint inside the stencil, creating a leaf design on his paper. When the paint is dry, staple several sheets of blank paper and another sheet of art paper to the paper with the leaf shape. Cutting through all thicknesses, cut around the painted leaf shape to create a leaf journal.

Falling Leaves

Watching and writing about falling leaves may inspire your little ones to express themselves through creative movement. Why not have a leaf ballet? To encourage everyone to participate, assist youngsters in creating leaf-decorated streamers. Have each child glue several of the pressed leaves prepared in "Pressing Leaves" on page 6 onto orange, yellow, or red crepe-paper streamers. Play a selection of instrumental music; then let the dance begin! Swing and sway! Let the wind blow today! We're falling leaves and we're on our way!

Fall Foliage Art Festival

Brighten up your room with these easy
and colorful art projects.

Cooperative Leaf Mural

Working together, your little ones can welcome autumn with this beautiful mural. Enlarge several of the leaf patterns on page 13 onto separate sheets of white bulletin-board paper. Divide the class into small groups. Provide each group with sponges, two colors of paint in tins, and one of the large leaf outlines. Direct the children in each group to completely sponge-paint their leaf using one of the colors of paint. When the first color is dry, have them sparingly sponge-paint the second color over the first. When the second color of paint is dry, outline each of the leaves using a wide-tipped, black marker. Cut out the leaves; then glue them to a length of bulletin-board paper. Add the title "Welcome Autumn!" to the mural; then display the mural in a hall for everyone to enjoy. Your youngsters are sure to receive lots of compliments on their cooperative creation!

Leaf Banners

Youngsters will be proud to take these beautiful leaf banners home to use as seasonal decorations. Using the pattern on page 12, prepare leaf-shaped templates. To make a banner, trace a template onto a 12" x 18" sheet of construction paper. Squeeze colored glue onto the resulting outline. When the glue is dry, color inside the leaf outline. Place the paper atop a second sheet of construction paper that is identical in color and size. Glue or staple the pieces together along the top. To prepare the banner for hanging, slide a three-foot length of yarn between the two sheets; then tie the ends of the yarn. It's a banner time of year!

10

Splatter-Painted Leaves

Your little ones are sure to be flattered when they receive compliments on these splatter-painted leaves. Place a sheet of newspaper inside a wide but shallow cardboard box. Dip the bristles of a toothbrush into diluted tempera paint. Hold the toothbrush several inches above the paper, positioning the toothbrush so that the bristles are pointing up and the head of the brush is tipped down toward the paper. Scrape a plastic knife over the toothbrush bristles, moving the knife away from your body. Move the toothbrush around as you splatter to cover as much of the paper as possible. When the paint is dry, trace leaf shapes onto the paper. Cut out the shapes; then mount them onto a black background.

Your little ones will also love using this splatter-painting technique to create reverse stencils. Using the leaves on page 13 as patterns, cut leaf shapes from cardboard. Place a sheet of plain newsprint in the cardboard box. Arrange the leaf shapes on the paper. Then, using the technique described, splatter-paint the entire piece of paper. When the paint is dry, remove the leaf shapes. Use the paper as wrapping paper for student-made gifts or as background paper for a fall display. What "autumn-matically" amazing artwork!

Fall Collages

Stock an art center with plenty of pressed leaves, twigs, acorns, seeds, and other natural items. Also supply the center with construction paper in fall colors, scissors, glue, and Styrofoam® meat trays or the bottom halves of cardboard pizza boxes. Encourage youngsters who visit the center to use the materials to design their own seasonal collages.

Leaf Rubbings

These colorful crayon rubbings of fresh, fall leaves are lovely enough for framing! For each child, you will need one 9" x 12" sheet of colored construction paper, one 8" x 5" piece of construction paper in a contrasting color, and one 4" x 7" piece of thin, white paper. To make a leaf rubbing and frame, set the white paper on top of a leaf. Rub over the paper with the side of a crayon until the leaf outlines appear on the paper. To make the frame, fold and staple each corner of the larger sheet of construction paper as shown. Center and glue the contrasting color of construction paper over the frame to create a mat. Center and glue the leaf rubbing to the center of the mat. Now you have a fine, fall print that is framed and ready for hanging. Fantastic!

Leaf Pattern

Use with *Red Leaf, Yellow Leaf* on page 8; "Leaf Journals" on page 9; and "Leaf Banners" on page 10.

Leaf Shapes

Use with "Seasonal Sorting" and "A Lovely Leaf Song" on page 7, "Leaf Manipulatives" on page 9, "Cooperative Leaf Mural" on page 10, and "Splatter-Painted Leaves" on page 11.

Booklet Pages

Use with " 'Where Is The Leaf?' Booklet" on page 8.

Where is

the leaf?

©1996 The Education Center, Inc.

1

Glue lid here.

in the box

2

on the dog

3

Glue tablecloth here.

under the table

4

above the cat

5

Glue child here.

behind me

child

lid

tablecloth

Family Ties

As you look into the faces of your students, you see the products of many different kinds of families—*nuclear, extended, adoptive, single-parent, blended,* and *foster* families. Regardless of the type, a *family* is "a group of people who have strong ties to one another." These ties are a result of their love and care for each other, their sharing of lives and living space, and their sense of belonging with one another. Use the following activities to help youngsters explore their family ties.

by Mackie Rhodes

What Is A Family?

Before beginning the activities in this unit, give yourself a mini–refresher course on the different types of families by reading *What Is A Family?* and *What Kind Of Family Do You Have?* by Gretchen Super (Twenty-First Century Books). Use the information and situations from the books to address sensitive questions concerning your own students' families.

My Family

Encourage each of your little ones to make a representation of his own family using this simple art idea. Gather several sizes of people-shaped cookie cutters. Provide a tray of tempera paint and a supply of construction paper. Have each child decide on the shape and size of cookie cutter that best represents each of his family members. Then have him dip the cutters into the paint and press them onto a sheet of construction paper. When the outlines have dried, he may use markers to personalize and embellish each outline. Have him write (or dictate) the name of each person on his paper. Across the top of the paper write "[Child's Name]'s Family." After the pictures are completed, the pages may be bound into a class book titled "Our Families." While sharing the book, encourage each of your students to tell something special about his family.

The Family Connection

Being part of a family means relating—or being connected—to your family members in a variety of ways. With this activity, your children can begin to understand some of the ways they are connected to their families. Ask each child to bring in a family photograph. Provide three 4" x 6" plain index cards for each child. Cut four 5" x 7" pieces of construction paper for each child to use as backings for his cards and family photo. Also cut a 2 1/2-foot-long strip of two-inch-wide ribbon for each child.

On each card, encourage each student to illustrate an activity he enjoys doing with members of his family. If desired, have each student write or dictate a sentence to describe each of his pictures. Mount each of these pictures and the family photo on one of the construction-paper rectangles. Attach the family photo about two inches from the top of the ribbon. Then connect the other pictures by attaching them to the ribbon at evenly spaced intervals. If desired mount a bow above the family photo and attach an adhesive-backed magnet to the back of it.

My Family Tree

With this family tree, each of your little ones will be popping with pride over the important place he has in his family. To begin, ask each child to bring in a small picture of himself (or photocopy his school photo). Duplicate a large supply of the leaf patterns on page 22 on green construction paper; then cut out enough leaves to correspond with the number of people in each child's family. Also duplicate a class supply of page 24 and the verse on page 22. For each child, fold a 9" x 12" sheet of construction paper in half. Glue a copy of the verse onto the center front of the folded construction paper. Next encourage each child to cut along the rectangular outline and color the picture of the tree on his copy of page 24. When he is finished, fold the paper in half so that the tree is on the outside. Cut along the indicated lines through both thicknesses to make a pop-up section. Next refold the picture with the tree on the inside. While folding, pull the pop-up section forward and crease it. (When the paper is unfolded, the pop-up section will separate from the rest of the page.) On separate leaf cutouts, have each child write (or dictate) the names of each of his family members. Help him glue his own leaf and picture onto the bottom part of the pop-up section. Then he may arrange and glue the other cutouts on the tree. To complete, fit the tree picture on the inside of the construction paper by nesting the pages together along the fold lines. Glue the two pages together, being careful not to glue the pop-up section.

The Unbroken Circle

Have each of your students make a necklace to represent the unending circle that is formed by his family. To begin, cut a supply of cardboard tubes into four-inch lengths. Then put the tubes and a variety of craft items in a center. Allow each child to decorate several tubes to represent members of his family. Then help him punch two holes near the top back of each tube. Encourage him to string his yarn through the holes in each tube. (Wrap one end of the yarn tightly with tape to make a needle for threading.) Tie the ends of the yarn together to make a necklace. Have each child wear his necklace during a discussion about family members. Talk about family members who have not been represented. For instance, you may point out that grandparents, aunts, uncles, and cousins are all part of the family circle.

Family Size

Find out from each of your students how many people live with him. Then ask your children to tell you how many people they think are needed to make up a family. After hearing their responses, teach the children the hand signs on page 23. Use the signs as you sing this song. When the verse about the number in his own family is sung, each child may stand and perform the hand signs.

(sung to the tune of "Ten In A Bed")

There were [ten] in a family,
And they all smiled and said,
"I love you. I love you."
Then they hugged and they hugged,
And they all felt so loved.
"I love you. I love you."

Repeat this verse—substituting the number *nine,* then *eight, seven,* and so on until you reach the number *one.* When you reach the verse for the number one, pause to ask your students whether a family can consist of only one person. If your children agree that one person constitutes a family, continue the song, adjusting the words to reflect the singular.

How Many Is A Family?

Help your little ones understand the broader scope of *family* by reading *One Hundred Is A Family* by Pam Muñoz Ryan (Hyperion Books For Children). Ask each student to brainstorm the many different types of families he belongs to. (These may include a *nuclear family, classroom family, church family, community family,* or any other group with whom he has common characteristics.)

To give students hands-on practice in counting and understanding the many dimensions of a family, gather a large supply of counters for this follow-up activity. Encourage each child to take one counter to represent each member of his family. Ask him to tell the number of people in his own family. Then have each child put one counter inside a circle to represent himself (add one for yourself, too). Count these to arrive at the number of people in your class family. Next create an extended family for your class by having each child add his other counters to the circle. Count the number of members in the extended class family. To continue, allow each child to add a counter to the circle to represent a schoolmate, neighbor, or community helper as a community family is created. How many families can your youngsters create? Count the members of each family as the type of family and number of members changes. How many is a family anyway?

Languages Of Love

Family members know one another so well that often they develop special ways to communicate with one another. Ask your students to think about the ways they communicate with their

My sister smiles at me.

Keisha

families. Discuss questions like "How many different ways does your family let you know that you are loved? Do they use only words? Does your entire family speak the same language? Are any special gestures or facial expressions used? Is sign language or body language [such as reaching out for a hug] used in your family? How do members of your family communicate other feelings, such as happiness, sadness, anger, or pride?" After discussing these questions, have each student draw a picture to depict a special way that a family member communicates love to her. Encourage each child to go home and show or tell her family members that she loves them.

Family Treasures

With this treasure chest full of valuable information, you can help each of your little ones tell about his family's special times or traditions. Decorate a large shoebox to resemble a treasure chest. Reproduce page 25 (after filling in the due date) for each child to take home. When all of the pages have been returned, place them in the treasure chest. During circle time remove one page at a time from the chest. Allow each child to add information and embellish stories as you read the information on his page. Then encourage him to tell the group about the attached picture. What treasured memories your little ones have to share with others!

My family likes to eat ____spaghetti____.

My family enjoys going to ____the park on the weekends____.

My family likes to play ____baseball____.

My family works together when we ____clean the house____.

The special times my family celebrates are ____birthdays and Christmas____.

My family plays together.

My family works together.

All Together

Your little ones can sort out their ideas about time spent with their families by participating in this categorizing activity. For each child, prepare a sheet of construction paper by drawing a line down the middle. On one side of the paper, write the words "My family works together." On the other side, write "My family plays together." Provide a variety of magazines, catalogs, and newspaper sales flyers. Also provide scissors and glue. Have the children cut out pictures to represent different work and play activities they do with their families. Then have them glue each of the pictures on the side of their construction paper with the type of activity it best represents. Encourage your children to tell about some of the pictures they selected.

Conflict And Compromise

Working together to resolve conflicts can help a family learn to listen to and accept one another. By role-playing and resolving typical family conflicts together, your little ones can learn important compromise skills to use during actual conflicts. Encourage your children to set up each of these conflict situations using props in the classroom. Have them assume the roles of the family members in each scenario. As the situation is played out, discuss possible solutions. Also examine the feelings of each person involved in the conflict.

But I wanted to build a zoo.

- You want to use the blocks to build a bridge for your cars. Your brother wants the blocks to build a zoo.

- You are watching your favorite movie at home. Your sister turns the movie off so she can watch the cartoon show that has just come on TV.

- Your sister is sitting in your favorite reading chair, but you want to use the chair now.

- Dad asked you to put your toys away. You're too busy playing with your kitchen set to put your other toys away.

- Mom wants you to feed the dog. You don't want to to help Mom now because you will miss some of your favorite TV show.

Always Available

Most of us have at least one family member who is always available to us—in good and bad times. Encourage your children to think about the people in their families who are always there for them. Ask them to remember times when they were happy about a certain occasion, wanting to hear a special story, upset over an argument with a friend, nervous about school, sick with a cold, lonely, or scared. Can they recall the people in their families with whom they were able to share these times? Encourage them to make cards of thanks for these special family members. Have each child write (or dictate) a brief message on his card. The security of a special loved one is so important to all of us!

When The Relatives Come

Who are your relatives? Do they ever visit your family? What does your family do when relatives visit? How do you feel when your relatives come? When they leave? Use these questions to prompt a discussion about relatives and the time spent with them. Then read *The Relatives Came* by Cynthia Rylant (Bradbury Press). Encourage your students to compare the events in the book to their own experiences. For additional discussion, ask students to tell about a good thing that happens when relatives visit. Also allow them to tell which relatives they enjoy spending time with. For further thought, pose the question, "Could a relative live with you?" To conclude have each child draw a picture depicting a day his relatives came.

A Family Lives Together

Give your little ones some lively listening fun using Hula-Hoops® and this simple tune. To begin, place the Hula-Hoops® on the floor to represent homes. Have your children form into groups of four or five. Explain that each group of children will make up one family. For this activity each family will pretend to live in a home (a Hula-Hoop®) together. Encourage each group to select a color or shape to be designated as its family name. Gather each family around its home. Then sing the song. As you sing, fill in the blank with each group's family name during its turn.

(sung to the tune of
"The More We Get Together")

The {name of color or shape} family lives
    together, together, together.
The {name of color or shape} family lives
    together—in a home.
They **jump** in the home, and out of the home.
    In the home, and out of the home.
The {name of color or shape} family lives
    together—in a home.

Provide variety in the song by changing the boldface word to another action word, such as *step, march, hop,* or *tiptoe.*

Family-Related Literature

Horace • Written by Holly Keller
• Published by Greenwillow Books

I Love My Family • Written by Wade Hudson
• Published by Scholastic Inc.

Octopus Hug • Written by Laurence Pringle
• Published by Boyds Mills Press, Inc.

Leaf Patterns
Use with "My Family Tree" on page 17.

Verse
Use with "My Family Tree" on page 17.

I have a special place in my own family.
I need my family, and my family needs me.
Open up this page with my family tree
To find that important person I call me!

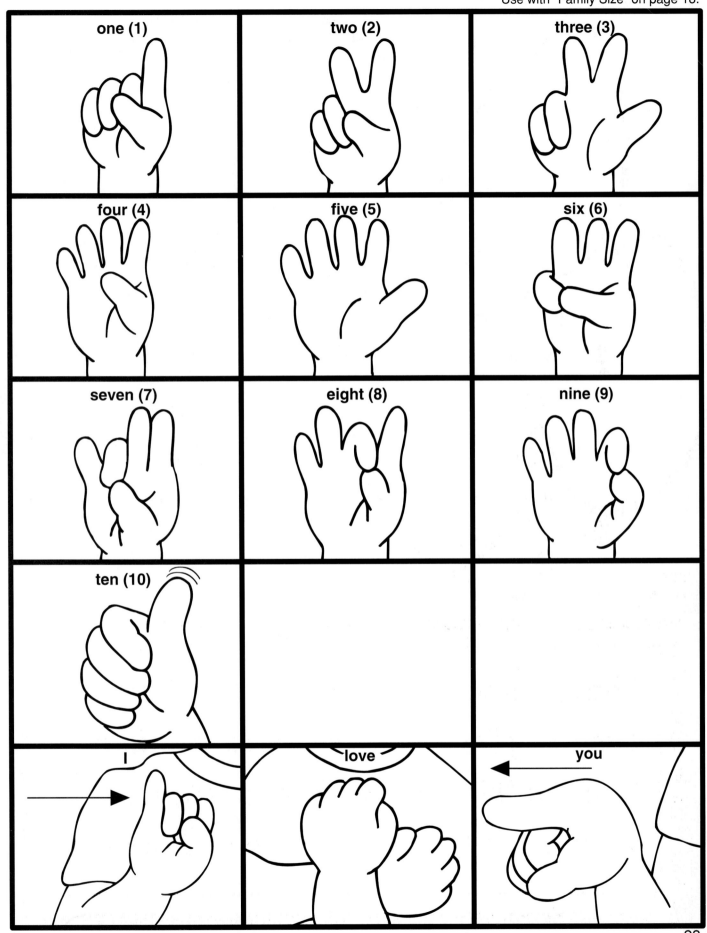

one (1)
two (2)
three (3)
four (4)
five (5)
six (6)
seven (7)
eight (8)
nine (9)
ten (10)
I
love
you

Tree Pattern

Use with "My Family Tree" on page 17.

cut line

cut line

Fold paper here.

Glue photo here.

Dear Family,
  We are talking about families at school. Each family has a treasury of special activities and times they share. Please help your child fill out this form. It will be used at school to help your child tell about your family's special times, things, and places. Please return it with your child by _____.
                                                                                      (date)

This treasure belongs to the _____ family.

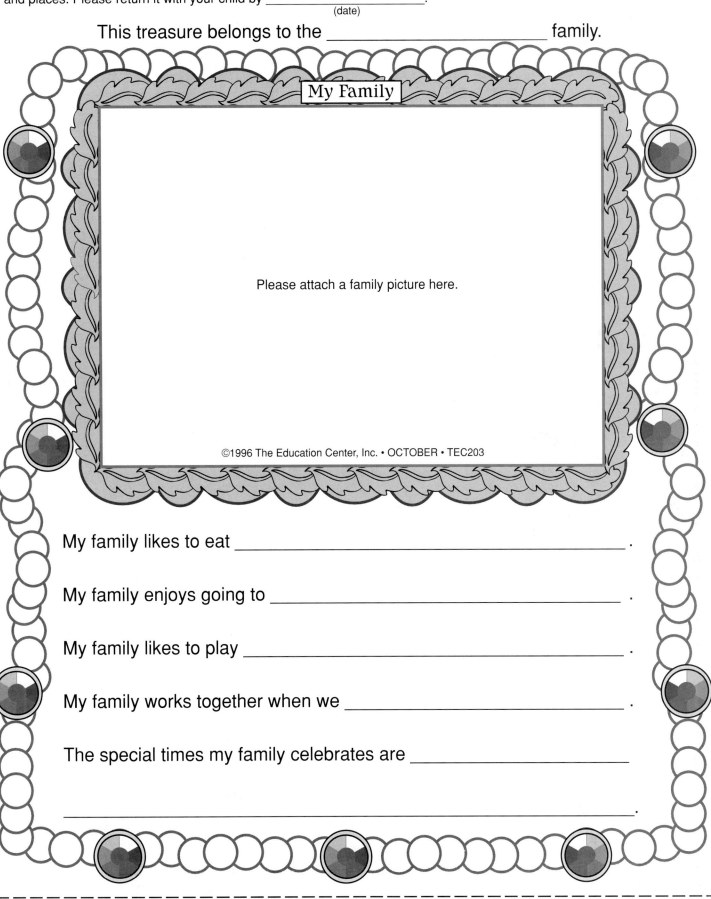

My Family

Please attach a family picture here.

©1996 The Education Center, Inc. • OCTOBER • TEC203

My family likes to eat _____.

My family enjoys going to _____.

My family likes to play _____.

My family works together when we _____.

The special times my family celebrates are _____

_____.

Fire Safety Is A HOT Topic!

Preventing fire and related injury is one of the most important topics you will share with your children all year. Use the ideas in this unit to help your little ones learn critical safety skills.

ideas contributed by Deborah Burleson and Ada Hamrick

Talk About It

Anyone who has ever been mesmerized by a glowing fire in a fireplace can easily understand why fire would fascinate a young child. Begin your fire-safety unit by asking youngsters to name some places they have seen fire, such as on lighted birthday candles, at campfires, or during space-shuttle launches on television. Discuss with children how fire can benefit people by providing heat and energy. Point out that fire can be a wonderful thing when it is used carefully.

Then discuss the dangers of fire. Have any of the youngsters seen TV news stories about a house or forest fire? How do they think such a fire might start? Point out that when fire is not handled carefully, it can easily get out of control. It can damage property and hurt people and animals. Ask students to brainstorm a list of all the things they've heard about fire safety. This discussion will give you an idea of what your youngsters already know about fire safety and what you need to emphasize.

Playing It Safe

Use this activity to focus attention on an important safety rule—never play with matches! First read and discuss *Matches, Lighters, And Firecrackers Are Not Toys* by Dorothy Chlad (Childrens Press®). Then place several toys and a book of matches on a tabletop so that all the children can see them. Ask a volunteer to come forward and point to the item that doesn't belong. Ask him to explain his reasoning. Guide all the children to recognize the importance of not playing with matches. Repeat the activity with another selection of toys and a cigarette lighter. Then teach little ones this poem to help them remember what they've learned.

Don't play with a match –it's not a toy.
You could start a fire–boy, oh boy!
A lighter can be dangerous, too.
These are not toys for me or you.

Only a grown-up should light a match.
I'll stick with playing "house" or "catch."
So this is what I have to say:
I'm going to play it safe today!

—Ada Hamrick

Dear Mom or Dad:
Please help me learn my address.
I'll need to know it if I ever need to call 911!

In case of emergency, dial
911

Dear Mom or Dad:
I'm so proud!
I practiced calling 911 today, and I was able to give my address!
Let me recite it for you.

In case of emergency, dial
911

It's An Emergency!

Despite precautions, fires and other emergencies do occur. It's important for youngsters to know what to do in the event of an emergency. Teach your little ones that their first priority if caught in a fire is to GET OUT and STAY OUT. If a child sees a fire or another emergency situation, he should report it to an adult, if at all possible. If no adult is available, youngsters should dial 911 (or the local emergency number).

Bring in some real telephones—minus the cords—for this activity. After a demonstration, have each youngster take a turn dialing the emergency number, giving her home address, and describing an imaginary emergency situation to the dispatcher (you). As each child takes her turn, note whether or not she knows her home address. After the activity, duplicate the parent notes on page 32 to send home with students.

Stop, Drop, And Roll

Ask your youngsters what they might do if their clothing caught fire. Explain that fire needs air to burn. Demonstrate this by lighting a small candle. Cover the burning candle with an inverted glass jar and have students watch as the flame goes out. Explain that in order to put out a fire on their clothing, they must keep the air away from the fire, just as the jar kept the air away from the candle flame. Running only provides more air for the fire to use. So instead of running, they will need to *stop, drop* to the ground, and then *roll* back and forth. Explain that rolling will squash the fire between their clothing and the ground, keeping the air away so that the fire will go out. Demonstrate this technique for the students; then ask each of them to try it. Have classmates cheer for each child as she successfully demonstrates the technique.

Crawl Low

Now that little ones know how to report a fire, teach them how to survive if they are caught in a burning building. Begin by emphasizing that their immediate goal is to GET OUT and STAY OUT. Then teach them how to *crawl low,* to help them find clearer air to breathe in a smoke-filled room.

To demonstrate just how low they must go, have little ones do a modified version of the limbo. Have a volunteer help you hold a yardstick as youngsters duck down to move beneath it. Lower the stick further for each round. For the final round, hold the stick very low and encourage little ones to crawl on their tummies—like little worms—to move under the stick. Explain to students that this is how they should crawl in a smoke-filled room.

Then have little ones practice their crawling technique on a classroom obstacle course. Set up a variety of chairs, tables, or play tunnels for children to crawl under and through. Ask students to pretend that each section of the course is a room in a smoke-filled house. The end of the course represents the door to outside and safety. Invite little ones to take turns crawling on their tummies through the obstacle course. Encourage classmates to cheer for each child as he safely exits the imaginary house.

The Sounds Of Sirens

Now that youngsters know what they can do to help themselves in the event of a fire, familiarize them with what will be going on around them if and when a fire occurs. The loud sounds made by fire engines, smoke alarms, and sirens can be very frightening for young children. Try this activity to get them accustomed to these sounds.

In advance, tape-record the sounds of a smoke alarm, a fire engine, or—if possible—your school's fire alarm. At circle time, discuss these sounds. Ask youngsters if they have heard any of these sounds; if so, what were their reactions? Give students a chance to express their fear or displeasure. Then explain the reasoning behind the high volume—to ensure that everyone knows there's an emergency. With the volume turned very low on your tape recorder, play the sounds you've recorded. What would happen if a real alarm were this quiet? Do students think they could hear it over the hubbub of a busy classroom? Would a quiet smoke alarm wake them from a sound sleep? Gradually increase the volume as you replay the tape several times, to get students used to the loudness of the sounds.

Fire-Drill Practice

Young children will need extra practice with your school's fire-drill procedures. If you made a recording of your school's fire alarm for "The Sounds Of Sirens" activity, use it for this classroom practice. Or ring a special bell to represent the fire alarm's sound.

Begin by discussing why fire drills are held at school. Then discuss the procedures your class will follow if the fire alarm is sounded. Have students line up; then walk them to the outside meeting place for your class. Demonstrate how you will count heads to be sure that everyone has arrived outside safely. Then return to the classroom. Ask students to pretend they are engaged in center-time activities. Explain that when you sound the pretend alarm, they should line up quickly and quietly. Do this several times. Then hold a practice fire drill—sounding the pretend alarm, lining up, and going outside to the meeting place. When you return to the classroom, reward your youngsters with a hearty congratulations and an assurance that they are ready for a real fire drill!

S-h-h-h-h

Fire Fighter To The Rescue!

In the event of a fire, a youngster may come face-to-face with a fire fighter dressed in full turnout gear, including a helmet, a face shield, and an oxygen hose. He may even have an axe in hand! That could be a frightening and intimidating sight. To familiarize your students with the appearance of a fire fighter, invite one to visit your classroom. Ask the fire fighter to come dressed in street clothes, but bring along his full gear. Ask him to put on his protective clothing and gear piece by piece, explaining why he wears each article. Have him speak to the children through the mouthpiece for his oxygen tank, so they can hear how his voice may sound in a rescue situation. Then have him remove each piece of gear so that students can see he is still a real person underneath. With the fire fighter's permission, choose a child volunteer to put on some of his clothing, such as his boots, coat, and helmet. The sight of a classmate wearing the oversized gear is sure to evoke giggles and make the equipment less intimidating.

Friendly Fire Fighter

Review the special clothing and equipment of a fire fighter with this song. If desired, use the flannelboard pieces on page 33 to accompany the song. First duplicate page 34 for later use. Then glue page 33 to a sheet of tagboard and laminate it. Cut out the pieces and attach the hook side of a strip of Velcro® to the fire-fighter figure. Place a bit of Sticky-Tac on the back of each remaining cutout. Have a child "dress" the fire fighter on a flannelboard as the class sings each verse.

"The Fire Fighter"
(sung to the tune of "The Wheels On The Bus")

The fire fighter wears [big black boots],
[Big black boots], [big black boots].
The fire fighter wears [big black boots],
When he fights a fire.

Continue the song by substituting other phrases, such as *a turnout coat, a special hat, heavy gloves,* and *an oxygen tank.*

Look At A Book

Share the pictures in these photo-illustrated books for a look at real-life fire fighters.

Fire Fighters
Written by Robert Maass
Published by Scholastic Inc.

Fighting Fires
Written by Susan Kuklin
Published by Bradbury Press

I'm Going To Be A Fire Fighter
Written by Edith Kunhardt
Published by Scholastic Inc.

29

Let's Be Fire Fighters!

Now that your youngsters know what to do and what will happen in the event of a fire, give them some opportunities to demonstrate that knowledge. Begin by inviting children to participate in dramatic play. Transform your dramatic-play area into a fire station for a few weeks. Stock the area with child-sized raincoats and rubber boots, toy fire-fighter helmets (available at party-supply stores or through catalogs), a length of garden hose, a bell, and perhaps a stuffed Dalmatian. For an exciting central focus to the center, create a fire engine from a large appliance box. Have the children assist you in painting the box to resemble a fire engine, including a ladder along one side. Use a pizza pan as a steering wheel. Youngsters will delight in dressing as fire fighters, tossing the hose in the back of the truck, and speeding to a burning building to save the day!

Our Big Book Of Fire Safety

When we have a fire drill, we have to line up fast.

A Big Book Of Fire Safety

Create a class big book to show off students' knowledge about fire safety. Give each child a sheet of chart paper. Ask him to draw a picture that illustrates one thing he has learned about fire safety. Write his dictation at the bottom of the paper. Then make a front and back cover for the book from red poster board. Print the title "Our Big Book Of Fire Safety" on the front cover. Enlarge and duplicate the Dalmatian pattern on page 34, color and cut it out, and glue it to the cover. Punch holes in the front and back covers to correspond with the holes in your chart paper; then bind the pages between the covers with metal rings. Read the finished book to the class; then add it to your classroom library. This hot book is sure to spark a discussion about fire safety every time it's opened!

Something To Write Home About

Fire safety is a topic that must be addressed at home, as well as at school. Duplicate the parent letter on page 35 for each child to take home. Encourage the students to have their parents fill out the checklist at the bottom of the letter. Ask them to return it to school to indicate they've discussed important fire-safety issues at home. Give each child an opportunity to discuss his home fire-safety procedures.

Dear Parent,

At school we have been discussing fire safety. Your child has learned some important safety skills, such as how to *stop, drop,* and *roll* if his clothes catch on fire and how to *crawl low* to avoid smoke inhalation during a fire. We've also practiced for a fire drill at school.

Please take some time to discuss important safety measures that apply at home. Knowledge of fire-safety procedures could save your child's life! After your discussion, please help your child fill out the checklist below and return it to school. We'll talk about each family's checklist to reinforce what the children have learned.

Name **Stephen Doughty**

Fire-Safety Checklist

✓ I know two ways to get out of my house:

Out the front door

through the garage. and

✓ My family has decided on a meeting place. It is:

At Amy's house, next door.

✓ We have tested the batteries in our smoke alarm.

✓ The local emergency number is posted near our telephone.

It is: **911**

Delightful Dalmatians

Have your youngsters noticed that wherever there are fire fighters, there seem to be Dalmatians? That's because the Dalmatian is the unofficial mascot—or good-luck charm—of fire fighters. Read about a Dalmatian in the book *Firehouse Dog* by Amy and Richard Hutchings (Scholastic Inc.) This selection with photo illustrations follows Hooper the dog and his fire-fighting friends through a day on the job.

After reading the story, invite youngsters to make firehouse dogs of their own. For each child, duplicate the Dalmatian pattern on page 34 on white construction paper. Have him color and cut out the pattern; then tape a craft stick to its back. Suggest that each child name his puppet. Then invite each child in turn to introduce his puppet and have it recite a fire-safety rule for the class. "Bow wow!" means "Never play with matches!"

Fire Chief Badges

Conclude your fire-safety unit by awarding each hardworking child a special fire chief's badge. Duplicate the badge patterns on page 34 on tagboard. For each child, cut out a badge shape. Invite the child to sponge-paint one side of the badge with silver tempera paint. After the badge dries, glue a child's school photo to its center. Using a permanent marker, print "Fire Chief" and the child's name on the badge. Use a piece of rolled masking tape to stick each child's badge to his shirt. Your youngsters will be glowing with pride!

Fire Chief

Maggie

Dear Mom or Dad:

Please help me learn my
 address.
I'll need to know it if I ever
 need to call 911!

In case of emergency, dial
911

©1996 The Education Center, Inc. • *OCTOBER* • TEC203

Dear Mom or Dad:

I'm so proud!
I practiced calling 911 today,
 and I was able to give my
 address!
Let me recite it for you.

In case of emergency, dial
911

©1996 The Education Center, Inc. • *OCTOBER* • TEC203

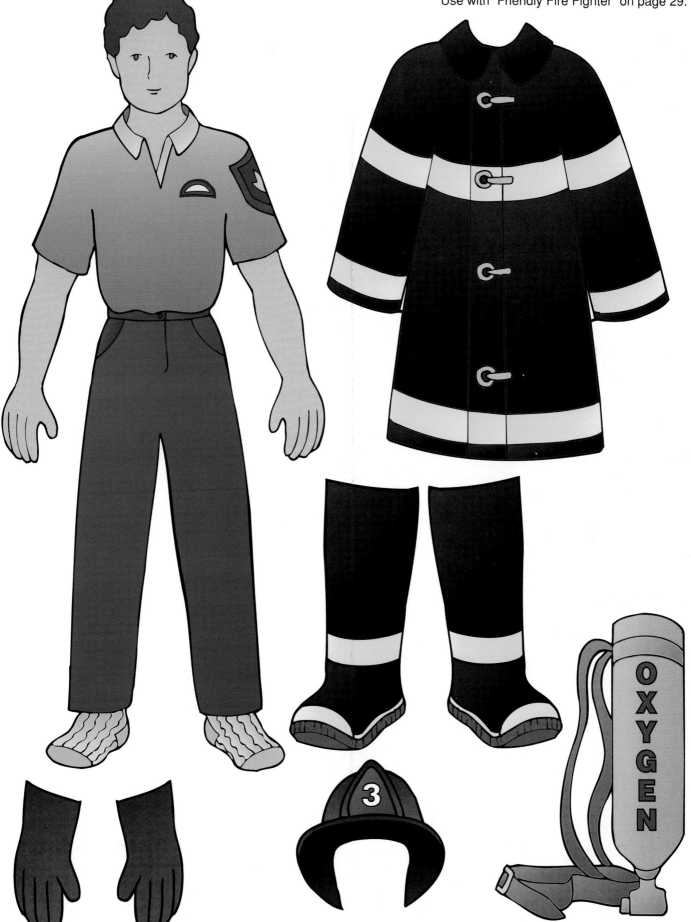

33

Badge Pattern
Use with "Fire Chief Badges" on page 31.

Dalmatian Pattern
Use with "A Big Book Of Fire Safety" on page 30 and "Delightful Dalmatians" on page 31.

Dear Parent,

At school we have been discussing fire safety. Your child has learned some important safety skills, such as how to *stop, drop,* and *roll* if his clothes catch on fire and how to *crawl low* to avoid smoke inhalation during a fire. We've also practiced for a fire drill at school.

Please take some time to discuss important safety measures that apply at home. Knowledge of fire-safety procedures could save your child's life! After your discussion, please help your child fill out the checklist below and return it to school. We'll talk about each family's checklist to reinforce what the children have learned.

Thank you!

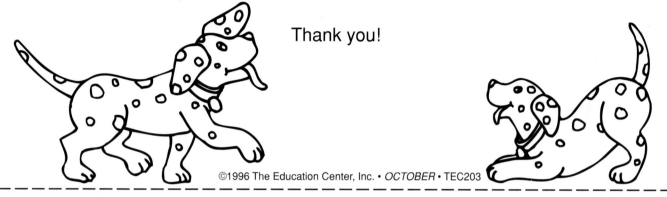

Name_____

Fire-Safety Checklist

_____ I know two ways to get out of my house:

_____ and

_____

_____ My family has decided on a meeting place. It is:

_____

_____ We have tested the batteries in our smoke alarm.

_____ The local emergency number is posted near our telephone.

It is: _____

Note To The Teacher: Use this parent letter with "Something To Write Home About" on page 31.

Simply Spiders

Quick, precise engineers. Efficient hunters and travelers. Intimidating features. Virtually harmless to humans. What creatures are these? Spiders—simply spiders! Delight youngsters with the opportunity to learn more about spiders with this simply spidery unit.

ideas contributed by Carol McPeeters, Mackie Rhodes, and Sarah Tharpe-Winchell

The Human Spider

Begin your study of spiders by inviting students to imitate some arachnid actions. Have youngsters form a human spider to help them understand the coordination it takes for a spider to move on eight legs. Whether long and thin or short and stubby, a spider's legs are attached to its body in pairs. To help youngsters understand what a pair is, explain to them that they each have two legs—a pair. Then invite four volunteers of approximately the same height to become part of a human spider. Have the children hold their hands behind their backs. Then, facing outward, have them form a small circle. Lower a large beanbag chair—the body of the spider—into the middle of the circle. (If a beanbag chair is not available, use a large laundry bag stuffed with towels). Have the students lean their backs against the beanbag to support it between them. To keep the bag from slipping down, suggest that they use their hands to support it from the bottom. Challenge the human spider to move across the room, keeping all its legs attached to its body. Repeat the activity to give each child the opportunity to become part of the human spider. It may not be Spider-man®—but it moves just like a spider can!

Supper Time!

Do your students know that spiders eat only liquids? Spiders use their strawlike mouths to suck the body fluids from their victims. Entice your youngsters to sup like spiders with this tasty temptation. In advance purchase or prepare a class quantity of juice or a flavored drink. For each child, make a straw-sized hole just below the seal-strip on a resealable plastic sandwich bag. Push a straw into the hole so that it reaches the bottom of the bag. To support the bags during pouring, place them upright, one at a time, in the bottom of a cutaway cereal box. Fill each bag halfway with juice; then seal it tightly. At snacktime, encourage students to suck the liquid out of their bags as spiders do their meals. Have them discuss what happens to each bag as the liquid is drained from it. Explain that, like the bag, the spider's food also collapses as the liquid is sucked from it.

Dragline

A spider spins a silk thread, called a *dragline,* behind itself wherever it goes. It relies on the dragline to help it escape from danger by dropping quickly out of reach of the threat. The spider can climb back along its dragline after the threat has passed. To prepare a dragline for your little arachnid actors to use, tape one end of a 30-yard length of yarn to a toilet-paper tube. Wrap the yarn around the tube. Slide the tube onto a narrow belt. Then arrange an obstacle course using chairs, tables, stools, plastic cones, and other small furnishings. Loosely fasten the belt around the waist of a volunteer with the tube of yarn (the dragline) positioned near the middle of the child's back. Explain that the child will crawl on the floor pretending to be a spider as he negotiates the obstacle course. Have another child hold the loose end of the dragline at the beginning of the course. As the spider moves, his dragline will unroll, leaving a trail along the obstacle course. At the end of the course, remove the belt from the child's waist. Have him wind the yarn back onto the tube as he retraces his path.

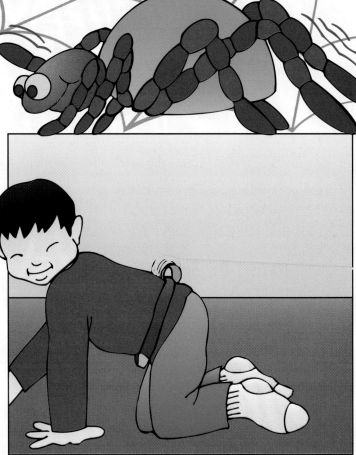

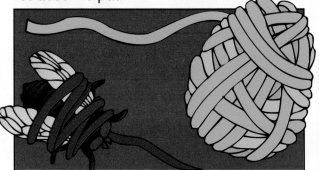

Spinning Surprises

Most female spiders spin a special kind of silk to enclose their eggs in an egg sac. Some spiders spin silk around their victims to prevent them from escaping. Have your youngsters spinning with delight with these super surprises. Provide a variety of rubber insects and small plastic eggs. Using arm-length pieces of yarn to represent silk, have each child wrap an insect or egg until it is covered. Secure the end of the yarn with a piece of tape. Place the wrapped items in a basket. Later encourage each student to make a selection from the basket, then unwrap the item. Ask him to try to guess the item before it is completely unwrapped.

The Scoop On Spiders

Did you know that...

... spiders are *arachnids,* not insects? Insects have six legs, while spiders have eight.

... all spiders spin silk? The spinnerets at the rear of their bodies spin the silk. Spiders use their silk as draglines, to make webs, to wrap their food, and to make egg sacs. Spiderlings use silk for *ballooning,* a special way of traveling through the air.

... most spiders have eight eyes? The number of eyes varies from species to species.

... all spiders have fangs? Poison flows through the tips of their fangs to stun their prey.

... most spiders are harmless? In North America, only six kinds of spiders are harmful to humans. These include four types of widows, the brown recluse, and the sack spider.

Spiders, Spiders Everywhere!

In corners and cracks, under rocks and grass—spiders can be found practically everywhere. But not all spiders are alike. Introduce your little ones to two kinds of common spiders—the house spider and the garden spider.

Spying On Spiders

Students will be ready to spy on some live spiders after reading *Spider Watching* by Vivian French (Candlewick Press). Using information from the book and this unit, engage students in a discussion about spiders. Then take a walk on both the inside and outside of your school building to look for spiders. If desired, have little ones use magnifying glasses for close-up examinations of the animals and their webs. As they make their discoveries, encourage youngsters to share their observations of spiders with the class.

Spiders At School

Provide youngsters with a firsthand opportunity to observe this fascinating creature by bringing a spider to school. Gently capture a spider using a small net, cup, or jar. If desired, capture both an indoor and an outdoor spider. Use a large jar with airholes in the lid to create a temporary home for the spider. Place the spider inside the jar along with a moist cotton ball, a small amount of gravel or sand, and a small branch. Encourage students to observe the spider without disturbing its home. Have them comment on its features and behavior. Ask them to look closely for the spider's dragline. Will the spider build a web? If it does, encourage children to describe the web. Keep in mind that spiders thrive in their natural environments—plan to release the spider the next day.

Spiders At Home

The house spider can be found almost anywhere indoors—in a corner, behind a door, above a window, or under the couch. The common garden spider can be found outdoors along the ground, in a tree, behind a bush, or on a fence. Where do you find spiders around *your* house? Pose this question to your students. After discussing the many places spiders can be found around a home, have students make a "Spiders At Home" booklet. Reproduce and cut apart a class quantity of pages 44 and 45. Have each student color the front and back covers to represent the outside of a house. For each booklet page, encourage him to write or dictate the name of a household item or location to complete each sentence. Then have him illustrate each sentence by drawing the items and pressing his fingers onto a stamp pad and then onto each page to create fingerprint spiders. Have the student draw eight legs on each spider. Invite the child to make a few fingerprint spiders on both covers, as well. Sequence the completed pages between the covers; then staple the booklet along the left side.

A spider is **over** the ___door___

A spider is **in** the ___basket___

Spiders At Home

Web Weavers

Explore the types of webs woven by the house spider and the garden spider—and do a little spinning of your own—with this activity.

A house spider builds the simplest type of web. A *cobweb* is a loosely woven, tangled mass of silk threads attached to walls, furniture, and other supports. In an open area of the room, have students help build a cobweb. On the floor, have them sit cross-legged with knees touching to form a circle. Encourage students to roll a ball of colored yarn back and forth across the circle to create a web. As each child receives the yarn, provide him with a piece of masking tape to secure it to the floor before passing the yarn to another child. When finished, leave the cobweb on the floor.

A garden spider builds the most complicated web—an *orb web*. This web has spokes extending from the center. Spiral lengths of silk connect the spokes. To build an orb web, have students position themselves in a circle as described earlier. Guide the children to pass the yarn to named classmates around the circle to form an octagonal shape. Have each child secure the yarn to the floor with masking tape before passing it to the next child. Next have students follow directions to pass the yarn across the circle to make the spokes of the web, cutting and taping the yarn as necessary. Continue until all the children have had a turn taping and passing the yarn. Then weave the yarn in and out of the web-spokes, taping it as necessary, to create a spiral from the middle toward the edges of the web. Leave both webs in place for the activities in "Insect Toss" and "Crawl Like A Spider."

Insect Toss

Your little ones will get all caught up in this game of Insect Toss! Invite each student to take a turn imitating the helpful spider that catches insects that are harmful to humans. Begin by preparing the insect cards on page 43. First duplicate the patterns on page 44 for later use. Then laminate and cut apart the insect cards on page 43. Tape a coin to the back of each card. Using the webs created in "Web Weavers," have a child role-play either a house spider or a garden spider resting at the side of her web. From a given distance, invite another child to toss the insects onto the web. Then have the spider gather and count the number of insects caught in her web. Next have the insect-tosser pretend to be the spider, and invite another child to toss the insects. Continue play so that every child has the opportunity to role-play a spider and toss insects.

Crawl Like A Spider

Invite students to practice spider movements around the webs built on the floor. Call out the type of web to be circled around—the cobweb or orb web. Then sing this song as students perform the actions.

(sung to the tune of "Ten Little Indians")

[Crawl, crawl, crawl] like a spider.
[Crawl, crawl, crawl] like a spider.
[Crawl, crawl, crawl] like a spider.
[Crawl] around your web.

Repeat the verse, replacing the action word with *jump, run, creep, sneak,* or *pounce.*

Just Hanging Around

These necklace spiders will be the perfect pets for students to take home and share with their families—they just need a place to hang around! To make a spider necklace, duplicate the spider body patterns on page 42 for each student. Have the child decorate the top and bottom spider bodies using cotton swabs dipped in paint. When the paint dries, help each child cut out the patterns along the outlines. To make legs for each spider, twist four pipe cleaners together at the middle. Tape the twisted part of the legs section to the back of the top spider body. Then turn the bottom spider body over. To make spinnerets, position and tape two one-inch straws so they extend slightly beyond the large end—the abdomen—of the bottom body pattern. Have the student string each end of a 26-inch length of yarn through a spinneret toward the end of the body. Glue the top and bottom body patterns together. Tie the yarn ends together to make a necklace. Have students wear the necklace as they sing this song. Then encourage children to share what they know about spiders with their families.

Can You Believe Your Eyes?

Jumping spiders! Students will wonder if they can believe their eyes when they make this pencil-top optical illusion. For each child, duplicate the pencil-top pattern on page 42. Have each child cut on the bold lines, then color the spider and the web. Help him fold the paper on the vertical line. Tape the eraser end of an unsharpened pencil to the back of the picture of the spider. Then fold the paper on the horizontal line so that the web covers the other side of the pencil. Tape all the edges together so that the end of the pencil is sealed inside the paper. Have each student hold the pencil between the palms of his hands and roll it quickly back and forth. Quick as a blink! Is the spider on or off its web?

Spiders And Cider

Although the sight of spiders may cause some of your youngsters to tremble, they won't be squeamish about this tasty spider treat. To make a spider snack, have a student push four pretzel sticks into opposite sides of a doughnut hole. Help him use a plastic knife to spread peanut butter on the top of the doughnut hole. Encourage him to count out eight M&M's® Mini Baking Bits, then place them on the peanut butter to represent the spider's eyes. Invite students to enjoy their spiders with cups of warm apple cider.

I'm A Spider

(sung to the tune of "Found A Peanut")

I'm a spider,
A friendly spider.
From my thread,
I hang around.
With my spinnerets
And my eight legs,
I crawl up
And then back down.

Super Spider Spins

Share these super spins on spiders to sharpen students' skills on fact and fiction.

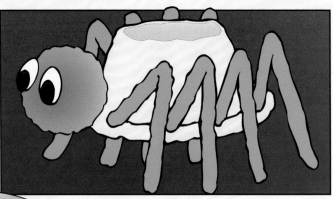

Miss Spider's Tea Party
by David Kirk
(Scholastic Inc.)

This tale portrays the congenial, but lonely, Miss Spider in need of only a few friends to join her tea party. Prior to reading the story, prepare tea and a class quantity of cupcakes decorated with icing to resemble spiderwebs. Read the story slowly, allowing students time to savor the delicious illustrations. Then ask them to tell what they think Miss Spider is—a house spider or a garden spider. Ask questions like "What does she eat? Are her meals like those of real spiders?" After the discussion, invite youngsters to a tea party. Provide a plastic spider ring for each child to wear as he enjoys his tea and cupcakes.

The Roly-Poly Spider
by Jill Sardegna
(Scholastic Inc.)

Read this delightful story once to students; then present it a second time to the tune of "The Itsy Bitsy Spider." Afterwards review the story. Have youngsters note the spider's change in size throughout the tale. Discuss the types of meals the roly-poly spider ate. Ask questions like "Are these the same types of things a real spider eats?" Encourage children to examine the pictures of the webs. How do these compare to the web of a garden spider? If desired, conclude by singing the story again.

I Love Spiders
by John Parker
(Scholastic Inc.)

Spiders are great—one and all! Read this book to youngsters to explore the different personalities, forms, colors, and other characteristics of spiders. Find out what characteristics each student would like to have if she could be a spider. In a center, provide a variety of craft items, such as pom-poms, egg-carton cups, pipe cleaners, wiggle eyes, tissue paper, paint, and glue. Encourage each child to create a spider to represent the kind she would like to be. Then have her write or dictate a sentence about her spider. Display the spiders and sentences with the title "I Love Spiders!"

More Spins To Share

Be Nice To Spiders
Written by Margaret Bloy Graham
Published by Harper & Row, Publishers

The Itsy Bitsy Spider
As told by Iza Trapani
Published by Whispering Coyote Press, Inc.

Anansi The Spider: A Tale From The Ashanti
Written by Gerald McDermott
Published by Scholastic Inc.

Additional Resources On Arachnids

Spider
Written by Michael Chinery
Published by Troll Associates

Amazing Spiders
Written by Claudia Schnieper
Published by Carolrhoda Books, Inc.

Keeping Minibeasts: *Spiders*
Written by Chris Henwood
Published by Franklin Watts

Pencil-Top Pattern
Use with "Can You Believe Your Eyes?" on page 40.

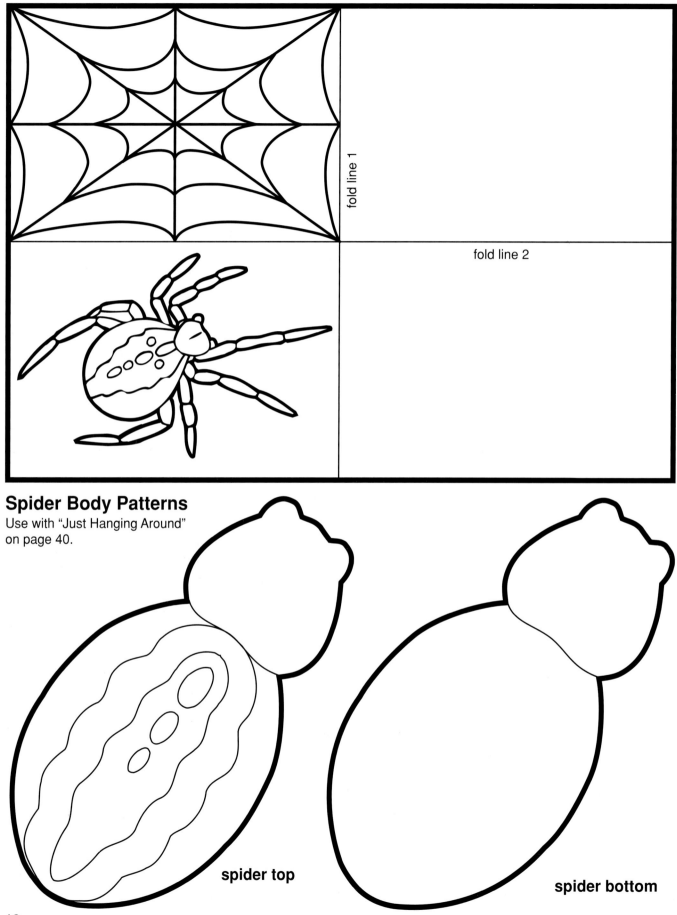

fold line 1

fold line 2

Spider Body Patterns
Use with "Just Hanging Around" on page 40.

spider top

spider bottom

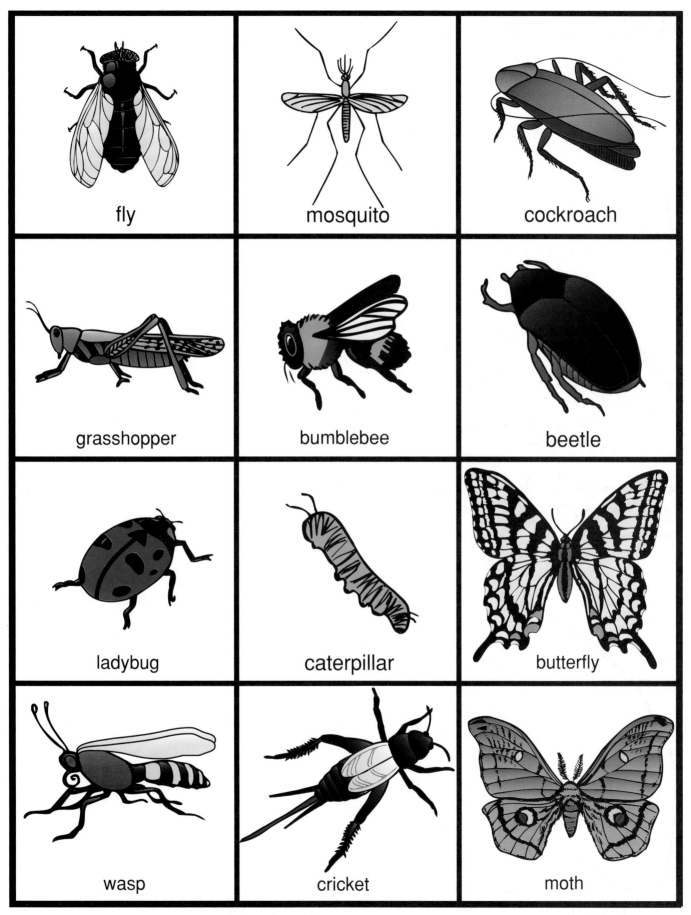

fly

mosquito

cockroach

grasshopper

bumblebee

beetle

ladybug

caterpillar

butterfly

wasp

cricket

moth

Front And Back Booklet Covers
Use with "Spiders At Home" on page 38.

Spiders
At Home

A spider is **over** the _____.

A spider is **in** the _____.

A spider is **on** the _____.

A spider is **under** the _____.

Any Way You Slice It...

Pizza is a great theme! You can't top this spicy subject for capturing little ones' interest. And there's plenty of learning in every slice!

by Ada Hamrick

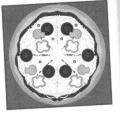

A pizza can be a circle.

We can be a circle.

Thank you for showing us how to make pizza.

Adrienne

Pizza Shapes

Begin this taste-tempting theme by bringing in two pizzas—one round and one rectangular. Ask youngsters to observe the shapes of the two pizzas; then take an instant photo of each one. Next cut the pizzas into slices as youngsters watch. Cut the round pizza into triangular pieces and the rectangular pizza into squares. Ask youngsters to identify each of these shapes. Then place an individual triangle and an individual square on separate serving plates and take an instant photo of each plate. Give each child a slice to enjoy.

After students finish eating, show the photos one at a time and review the four shapes—circle, rectangle, triangle, and square. Then divide the class into four groups. Assign each group a different shape to imitate. Have the students in the circle group lie down on a carpeted area to form a circle with their bodies. Take an instant photo of the group forming the circle. (You may need to stand on a chair to achieve the correct angle.) Ask the other groups to use their bodies to form their assigned shapes and take an instant photo of each one. Use all the photos to create a class book titled "Pizza Shapes." On sheets of construction paper, mount the photos of the corresponding shapes of pizzas and students; then program each page similarly to the one shown.

Visiting The Pizza Man

Many of your youngsters have probably visited a pizzeria or had pizza delivered to their homes. Learn more about the people who make and serve pizzas by reading the book *Pizza Man* by Marjorie Pillar (HarperCollins Children's Books). This photo-illustrated book with simple text will take youngsters through the day with a pizzeria worker as he does everything from mixing dough to assembling take-out boxes. Then plan a field trip to a local pizza restaurant or delivery center. You might even arrange to taste some free samples during your tour!

After your visit, be sure to assist the students in writing thank-you notes to the restaurant manager. To create a pizza-shaped note for each student, fold a sheet of tan construction paper in half. Trace a circle and cut it out, leaving a small strip of the fold uncut. Then ask each child to decorate the front of the note to resemble a pizza with her favorite toppings. Write the child's dictation for her thank-you message inside; then have her write her name below it. Now that's a note in good taste!

A Pizza Poem

This transparency tale will delight your youngsters. To prepare, use Vis-à-Vis® markers to illustrate seven transparencies for the overhead projector as shown. Be careful to make sure the illustrations line up when the transparencies are stacked, so that all the pizza toppings fall within the pizza outline and the smiles fall within the outlines of the faces. Stack them in order, with number 1 on the bottom and number 7 on the top. Use a hole puncher to punch two holes along the top edge of the stack. Bind the transparencies together with two metal rings. When you are ready to perform the poem for your little ones, set up the overhead projector and place only sheet number 1 on the lighted surface. As you read through the poem, flip over each sheet to overlap the previous one.

If you do not have access to an overhead projector, use clear sheet protectors in a three-ring binder. Cut open four sheet protectors along the outer and bottom edges. From one sheet protector, cut away one layer completely, to make a single thickness. Illustrate the seven resulting clear pages as shown. (Be sure that the illustrations overlap correctly.) Place the sheets in a three-ring binder. Perform the poem for your youngsters by holding the open binder and turning over the sheets one at a time, beginning with number 1 at the back and ending with number 7 at the front.

After learning the poem, little ones will enjoy using the transparencies as an individual or partner activity.

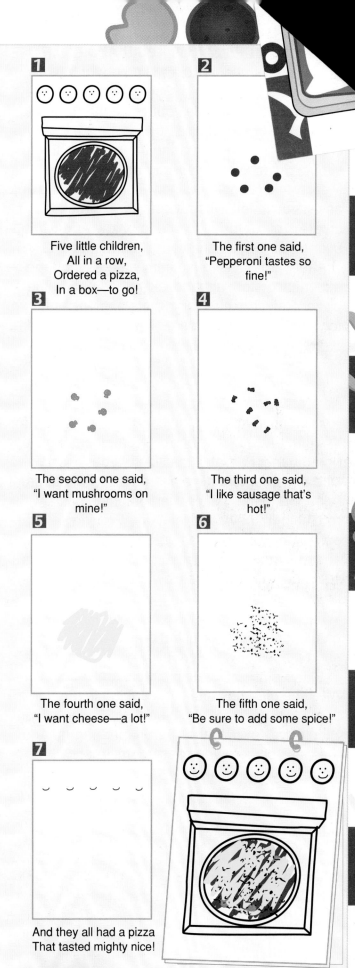

1
Five little children,
All in a row,
Ordered a pizza,
In a box—to go!

2
The first one said,
"Pepperoni tastes so fine!"

3
The second one said,
"I want mushrooms on mine!"

4
The third one said,
"I like sausage that's hot!"

5
The fourth one said,
"I want cheese—a lot!"

6
The fifth one said,
"Be sure to add some spice!"

7
And they all had a pizza
That tasted mighty nice!

Pizza! Pizza! Write All About It!

All this talk about pizza will no doubt have your youngsters hungry for a slice or two. So plan a pizza party to conclude your pizza theme. Bring in one or two boxes of pizza mix, depending on your class size. Before preparing the pizza, read the simple rhyming story, *Pizza Party!* by Grace Maccarone (Scholastic Inc.). Then have little ones assist you in following the package directions to create a pizza for everyone to enjoy. Add whatever toppings you and your students would like.

Afterward have youngsters write a language-experience story about cooking and eating the pizza. Have the children dictate sentences for you to write on the chalkboard. Then help the children organize the sentences to reflect the correct sequence of events. Copy the sentences onto sheets of chart paper and have pairs of students illustrate each step.

Then have students help you make a cover for this giant-sized class book. Cut a piece of bulletin-board paper to match the size of your chart paper. Use a marker to outline a large pizza with a crust edge. Fill in the "sauce" portion of the pizza with red tempera paint and let it dry. Provide several cut vegetables, such as green peppers, onions, and mushrooms. Invite each youngster to dip a cut vegetable into a shallow container of tempera paint, then print with it on the pizza drawing. When the vegetable prints have dried, squiggle glue over the pizza illustration. Give the children short pieces of white or yellow yarn to "sprinkle" onto the pizza to resemble mozzarella cheese. After the glue has dried, cut out the letters for the title "Making Pizza" and glue them on the cover. Staple the cover to the chart-paper pages. Add the class book to your classroom library.

We put tomato sauce on our pizza.

Pizza Puzzles

Help students practice sorting skills with this appetizing center. Prepare several pizza-shaped puzzles by tracing and cutting 12-inch circles of manila paper. Use crayons or markers to decorate each circle to resemble a pizza. Draw lines across each cutout to resemble slices on a pizza. On each pizza, affix a sticker to each slice that fits into a common category. For example, one pizza might feature stickers with a farm theme; another pizza might have letters of the alphabet. Cut the slices apart on the lines. Laminate all the slices and store them in a delivery box donated by a local pizza shop. To use the center, a child removes all the slices from the box and sorts them by category; then he reassembles the pizzas.

Great "Pizzas" Of Literature

Curious George And The Pizza
by Margret Rey and Alan J. Shalleck
Houghton Mifflin Company

Pizza For Breakfast
by Maryann Kovalski
Morrow Junior Books

Little Nino's Pizzeria
by Karen Barbour
Harcourt Brace Jovanovich

How Pizza Came To Queens
by Dayal Kaur Khalsa
Scholastic Inc.

OODLES OF NOODLES

Pasta comes in so many shapes, sizes, and colors. Use some noodles to get little ones involved in math, art, science, and language. The "pasta-bilities" are endless!

by Ada Hamrick

Where Does Spaghetti Come From?

Begin your pasta theme with a hands-on experience. Show the children a box of spaghetti noodles from the grocery store. Ask them if they know where spaghetti comes from. Then explain that pasta is usually made by making a dough from flour, eggs, and water, with other ingredients sometimes added to give the pasta a different color or flavor. Share the big book *Pasta, Please!* by Melvin Berger, published by Newbridge Communications, Inc., for more information on how commercial pasta is made. (The big book is available from Newbridge at 800-867-0307.)

If you have access to a pasta machine, bring it in and have little ones assist you in preparing some pasta. Use a recipe included with the machine for best results. Demonstrate how pasta can be formed into different shapes by using various dies on the machine. If you can't make pasta in the classroom, purchase some dried pasta in a variety of shapes and colors. Ask children to name the different types of pasta they may have eaten, such as macaroni, ravioli, egg noodles, or alphabet-shaped noodles.

The Story Of Spaghetti

Now that little ones know the origin of noodles, get them involved in cooking a popular pasta dish. Cook a batch of spaghetti with tomato sauce for the class to enjoy. Begin by giving each child a strand of dried spaghetti to hold. Ask student volunteers to describe the dried spaghetti. As the children watch, place the noodles into a pot of boiling water. (As always, exercise caution when using electrical appliances in the classroom.) After the spaghetti is cooked, drain it, rinse it with hot water, and let it cool until just warm. Give each child a strand of cooked spaghetti to hold. Have student volunteers describe how the texture of the spaghetti has changed. Then serve each child an individual portion of the spaghetti with heated tomato sauce. Be sure to provide plenty of napkins for this messy but delicious treat!

After everyone has finished her spaghetti, gather the children in your circle area. Have them dictate a language-experience story describing the preparation of the spaghetti and sauce. Encourage each child to contribute her thoughts to the story. Display the finished story on a classroom wall throughout your pasta theme.

What's The Magic Word?

Sometimes whipping up a spaghetti dinner doesn't go so smoothly. For the story of some pasta-making gone awry, read *Strega Nona* by Tomie dePaola (Scholastic Inc.). Once children have heard this tale several times, they'll enjoy chanting the magic words that help operate Strega Nona's magic pasta pot. To extend students' enjoyment of the story, have them create these magic pasta pot pictures.

Provide each child with a sheet of drawing paper, a four-inch square of black construction paper, scissors, crayons, glue, and several lengths of white yarn. Invite each child to cut the black paper into the approximate shape of Strega Nona's pasta pot; then have him glue the pot cutout onto the drawing paper. Have him draw Big Anthony and Strega Nona standing near the pot. Encourage him to glue the yarn strands onto the pot to resemble the overflowing pasta in the story. To complete the project, have each child make up his own magic words that will make the pasta pot boil. Write his dictation above his illustration. Display all the pictures on a bulletin board with the title "What's The Magic Word?"

Pasta Patterns

The magic word for math practice is "pasta." Show the children a variety of dried pastas. Include several different types and some different colors. Pour all the different pasta into a large container. Ask small groups to work together to sort the pasta by color, shape, or size. Then encourage the children to use the dried pasta for patterning practice. Provide a strip of card stock for each child. Have her arrange several pieces of pasta on the strip to create a pattern, such as *macaroni, shell, wheel, macaroni, shell, wheel.* When she is satisfied with her pattern, have her glue the noodles in place. Encourage each child to share her pattern with the other students in her group.

Noodle Necklaces

Couple patterning practice with fine-motor skills when you invite students to string pasta to create noodle jewelry. In advance, color some rigatoni in a variety of colors. Place the noodles into shallow pans of diluted tempera paint. Stir to coat the noodles well. Then place them on sheets of newspaper until dry. (You could use any variety of pasta that would be easy for children to string. If you are able to find colored pasta that will work well, omit the painting step.) Ask each child to string the noodles onto a 36-inch length of sturdy yarn in a pattern of her choice. When she has covered about three-quarters of the yarn length, tie the remainder of the yarn into a knot and slip the necklace over the child's head. Your youngsters will be proud to wear these pasta creations!

Please, Mr. Magic Pot,
Give me noodles that are hot!

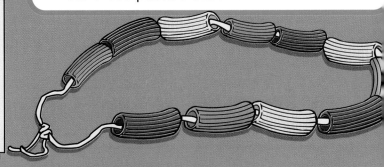

The Pasta Players

Use pasta to inspire your young musicians. Have each child use some dried pasta to create a rhythm instrument. Provide each child with a small lidded container such as a margarine tub, potato-chip can, or clean milk carton. Have her partially fill the container with pasta; then place a plastic top on the container or staple it securely closed. Encourage children to explore the sounds made by shaking their instruments. Then invite them to shake along to "The Pasta Chant." Ask a neighboring class if they'd like to hear a performance by your Pasta Players!

Crunchy Art

When your Pasta Players are all played out, remove the somewhat-crushed contents from the shakers. Place the crushed pasta into zippered plastic bags. Invite each child to use a small rolling pin or toy hammer to further crush the pasta pieces. Place the crushed contents into old salt shakers or glitter containers with perforated tops. Provide each child with a sheet of construction paper, glue, and some whole pasta pieces. Have each child create a picture by gluing the whole and crushed pasta on his paper. The texture of the pasta will add just the right touch to this "pasta-tively" pretty project!

The Pasta Chant

Pasta's delicious!
Oh, what a treat!
If you like pasta,
Just shake to the beat!

Pasta for breakfast,
Pasta for lunch,
I like pasta—
I like it a bunch!

Pasta for dinner,
Pasta for snack,
Oh no! I'm having
A pasta attack!

S'ghetti 'n' meatballs,
Macaroni and cheese,
Noodles with chicken soup,
Or even with PEAS!

Pasta's delicious!
Oh, what a treat!
If you like pasta,
Just shake to the beat!

A Pasta Feast

Conclude your pasta theme with a pasta-dish taste test. Ask several parents to prepare and bring in a pasta dish. Encourage them to prepare different types of dishes such as pasta salads, Italian specialties, noodle soups, or desserts such as *kugel*. Then invite your youngsters' parents to come to school for the Pasta Feast. Have each parent and child sample each dish and determine a personal favorite. Ask each parent who donated a dish to send in the recipe. With their permission, photocopy the recipes; then bind the copies into individual "Pasta Feast Recipes" booklets for each child to take home.

POP... POP... POPCORN!

Here's a topic that's just bursting with possibilities! Check out this sizzling selection of popcorn activities to get your little ones hoppin' and poppin' about learning!

by Ada Hamrick

A FEAST FOR THE SENSES

Can you hear the oil sizzling? Can you smell that delightful scent filling the air? Have your youngsters explore the five senses as they pop some popcorn. On the first day of your popcorn theme, bring in an electric skillet or popcorn popper, an extension cord, a king-size bedsheet, some popcorn kernels, and some oil. Spread the sheet in your circle area. Invite your students to sit well back from the edges of the sheet.* Then ask them to close their eyes as you prepare a surprise. Encourage the students to concentrate on what they can hear and smell while their eyes are shut.

Place the popper in the center of the sheet and turn on the heat. Pour in some oil. When the oil begins to sizzle, sprinkle in some popcorn kernels and periodically shake the pan. Leave the lid off. Invite students to open their eyes. Observe as your fascinated youngsters watch the popcorn hop right out of the pan onto the sheet! After a few kernels have popped, put the lid on the popper.

When all the kernels have popped, serve each child a small helping in a paper cup. (Add butter and salt, if you wish.) Ask students to concentrate on how the popcorn feels and tastes. After everyone has finished this snack, invite the children to describe the popcorn-popping experience. On a large sheet of chart paper, write the headings "Hear," "Smell," "See," "Feel," and "Taste." Have the students recount what they heard, smelled, saw, felt, and tasted during the experience. Encourage descriptive vocabulary as you write the students' sentences under each category.

Hear
I could hear the frying sound.
Smell
It smelled buttery.
See
I could see the corn pop.
Feel
It felt crunchy in my mouth.
Taste
It tasted salty.

*NOTE: Extra supervision will be helpful during this activity so that the children remain at a safe distance from popping kernels or oil. Explain that this science experiment is an exception and that popcorn poppers should never be used without lids.

POP MUSIC

Help youngsters recall the popcorn-popping experience when you teach this tune.

THE POPCORN SONG

(sung to the tune of "Down By The Station")

In the popcorn popper,
Kernels go ker-plink.
I can smell it cooking—
Almost done, I think!

See the popcorn popping,
Fluffy and so white.
Pop! Pop! Yum! Yum!
Tastes just right!

Kevin Piel Carly Juan Hannah

Sally LaJames

Carlos Josh

Beth

STRINGING THEM ALONG

A popcorn string is a wonderful thing—for small-motor practice! A few days in advance, pop a quart or two of popcorn, and allow it to sit uncovered. On the day of the activity, provide each student with a blunt, plastic needle that has been threaded with a length of dental floss. Invite your little ones to string the stale popcorn onto the floss. Place the finished strands on the trees near your classroom to provide food for birds.

Then create a paper popcorn string for your classroom. Provide each child with a large sheet of finger-paint paper and some white tempera paint. (Add a small amount of dishwashing liquid to the paint to make cleanup easier.) Invite each child to finger-paint on the paper; then let it dry. After the paint is dry, use a permanent marker to outline the shape of a puffy piece of popcorn on each paper. Ask each child to follow your line as best he can to cut out his piece of popcorn. Use the permanent marker to label each cutout with the child's name. Then have each child use a hole puncher to punch a hole at the top of his cut-out. Thread a long length of brightly colored yarn through the hole in each piece, and knot the yarn at equal intervals to create a paper popcorn string. Display the string as a bulletin-board border or door decoration during your popcorn theme.

POPCORN PRETENDING

Get your youngsters moving when you invite them to imitate popcorn kernels in a giant popcorn popper. Use chalk or masking tape to outline a large square or circle on your classroom carpet. Encourage all your youngsters to find a space inside this imaginary popper as you "pour" the kernels into the pan. Have them crouch down to imitate the unpopped kernels. Pretend to insert a giant plug into the wall outlet. As the imaginary heat rises, ask students to pretend they are getting hotter and hotter. Encourage students to jostle around inside the popper as you "shake" the kernels in the pan. When each popcorn kernel is so hot that she can no longer stand it, have her "pop" into a standing position. When all the kernels have "popped," ask students to imagine that they are being coated with melted butter and sprinkled with salt. Then invite them to exit the popper one by one as you select and "gobble" each piece of popcorn.

KEEP ON MOVIN'...
with these musical selections:

"Popcorn"
Sung by Greg and Steve
We All Live Together Vol. 2
Youngheart Records

"Popcorn"
Sung by Raffi
The Corner Grocery Store
Troubadour Records

COLORFUL KERNELS

Provide fine-motor practice and help students practice sorting skills with some colored popcorn. Purchase a package of colored popcorn kernels and obtain an empty egg carton to create this center. In advance, paint the bottoms of the egg cups to correspond with the colors of the popcorn kernels. Allow the paint to dry. Place a small handful of colored popcorn kernels into a lidded container.

To use the center, a child opens the container of kernels and spreads them on a tabletop. He picks up each kernel and drops it into an egg cup painted with the corresponding color. If desired, have the child use a pair of tweezers to pick up the kernels. You may wish to make several sets of cartons and kernel containers so that more than one child can use the center at a time.

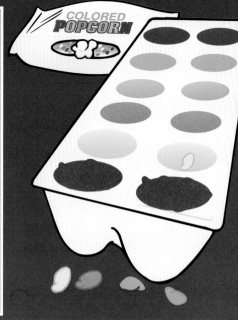

A "NUMMY" NUMBERS GAME

Help youngsters practice numeral identification with this game. Ask a local movie theater to donate a few small popcorn boxes. Then cut out a number of puffy popcorn shapes from heavy white paper. Program each cutout with a numeral that you'd like your students to learn to identify. Laminate the cutouts for durability.

To play the game, distribute a popcorn box to each student in a small group. Place all the popcorn cutouts facedown in a pile. The first player draws a cutout from the stack and attempts to identify the numeral printed on it. If correct, he may place the cutout in his box. If he is incorrect, he places the cutout at the bottom of the stack and the next child takes his turn. When all cards have been drawn, have each player count the popcorn pieces in his box. Vary the game by programming more cutouts with number words or sets or letters of the alphabet.

SNACKTIME, STORYTIME

Now that your little ones are popcorn experts, reward them with a snack of the fluffy white stuff! Pop a large batch of popcorn and give each child a cup of corn to munch. For added fun, provide a variety of toppings for students to sprinkle on their popcorn, such as butter flavoring, salt, Parmesan cheese, garlic salt, or cinnamon sugar. While students are munching, read aloud one of these "pop-ular" popcorn stories:

The Popcorn Dragon
Written by Jane Thayer
Illustrated by Lisa McCue
Published by Scholastic Inc.

Popcorn
Written & Illustrated by Frank Asch
Published by Putnam Publishing Group

Good Night! Sleep Tight!

Let the learning bug bite when you settle down for these across-the-curriculum ideas about bedtime, nocturnal animals, and the night sky. Host a pajama party for your little ones and their bedtime buddies as a dreamy end to this sleepy-time topic.

by Ada Hamrick

Pack A Pillowcase

Introduce your students to the subject of nighttime with a pillowcase puzzler. Place several night-related objects in a pillowcase. You may wish to include a toothbrush, pajamas or a small blanket, a book, a stuffed animal, and a star of some kind (perhaps one that you've created with paper, glue, and glitter or a star-shaped item such as a sponge or cookie cutter). Gather children together and show them the pillowcase. Explain that inside the pillowcase are several clues to your new topic of study. Remove the items one by one from the pillowcase. Invite youngsters to guess what all the items have in common. Guide students to the discovery that they'll be learning about night-time.

Then give little ones an opportunity to discuss the subject of night. Have volunteers explain their bedtime routines, tell about changes in the sky, or relate fears that accompany the darkness. Finish up your introduction by sharing the beautiful picture book *Night Is Coming* by W. Nikola-Lisa (Scholastic Inc.).

Time For Bed, Sleepyhead

Bedtime will be math time when you send home the parent project on page 62. Request that students discuss their bedtimes with their parents and complete the reproducible with their parents' guidance. When students return the assignments, create a graph to compare their bedtimes. Sketch a simple graph on a large sheet of bulletin-board paper. Write the title "When Do We Go To Bed?" at the top of the graph; then list the bedtime responses in a row across the bottom. Provide each child with an index card upon which to write his name. Assist each child in using Sticky-Tac or a rolled piece of masking tape to attach his name card to the graph in the space above his bedtime. Use a demonstration clock to familiarize the children with each bedtime, emphasizing the concepts of *earlier* and *later.* Then discuss the results of the graph, emphasizing the concepts of *more, fewer,* and *equal* numbers of students.

"Ten In A Bed"

Bring in some king-size sheets to help your little ones act out a favorite song about an overcrowded bed. Begin by teaching your youngsters the traditional song, "Ten In A Bed." Then create a giant sleeping bag from two, old, king-size flat sheets. Use wide masking tape to attach the sheets along two adjacent sides, creating a sleeping-bag shape with an open top and side. Have ten student volunteers snuggle into the sleeping bag. Then have your other students sing the song as your little actors perform the movements, rolling toward the open side of the sleeping bag on cue. Repeat the activity until all children have had a turn in the sleeping bag.

At Bedtime
(sung to the tune of "The Wheels On The Bus")

At bedtime, do you brush your
 teeth,
Brush your teeth, brush your
 teeth?
At bedtime, do you brush your
 teeth—
Each and every night?

A Sleepy-Time Tune

Review bedtime routines with your little ones when they sing and act out this song. Ask students to mime brushing their teeth each time that phrase is sung. Continue the song by substituting other phrases and their accompanying motions, such as *wash your face, put on jammies, get in bed, read a book, hug your teddy,* and *go to sleep.*

There were ten in the bed,
And the little one said,
"Roll over! Roll over!"

There Are Nightmares In Our Classroom!

Bedtime isn't all fun and games. Nighttime may be a scary time for some children. Read aloud *There's A Nightmare In My Closet* by Mercer Mayer (Dial Books For Young Readers). Then give your students a chance to discuss bedtime fears and apprehensions.

Follow up your discussion by creating a bulletin board of not-so-scary nightmares. Begin by providing each child with a sheet of white art paper. Drop a small amount of black tempera paint in the center of each child's sheet of paper. Have him fold the paper in half and press from the fold outward to spread the paint. Open the papers and allow the paint to dry. Then provide several colors of neon glue, such as Elmer's® GluColors™. Invite students to squeeze the glue onto the black free-form shapes to create facial or body features for their nightmares. Sprinkle clear glitter on the glue; then shake off the excess. Allow the glue to dry. Give each child a sheet of colored construction paper. To depict a closet door, have him draw a doorknob and label the sheet with his name. Mount the dried nightmares on the bulletin board. Staple each child's construction-paper door over his picture, so that it opens to reveal his nightmare creation. Title the board "Nightmares In Our Closets."

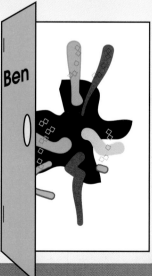

Ben

Creatures Of The Night

While little ones are tucked in bed, some critters are out and about. Introduce your students to some nocturnal animals with a good nonfiction book such as *A Picture Book Of Night-Time Animals* by Grace Mabie (Troll Associates). Then use the pictures of nighttime animals on page 63 to give students practice with classification skills.

Duplicate the animal cards on tagboard. Color the animals; then laminate them for durability if desired. Cut the cards apart. Then invite small groups of children to classify the animals into groups by various attributes. Students may choose to group the animals by size, number of legs, body coverings, or ways they travel (on the ground or in the air). Store the cards in a zippered plastic bag and keep them available at your science center for further exploration.

Firefly Fun

Which insects like to come out to play in the dark? Fireflies, of course! Share *The Very Lonely Firefly* by Eric Carle (Philomel Books). Your little ones will love the flashy ending! After reading the book, let youngsters imitate these evening insects. Give each child a small flashlight. Turn off the classroom lights and play a selection of classical music. (How about "Moonlight Sonata"?) Let your young fireflies flit, flutter, and flash in a large open space. Encourage them to blink messages to one another with their flashlights. Come on, fellow fireflies—it's time to play!

Fingerprint Fireflies

If your little ones are firefly fans, they're sure to light up when you introduce this art project. Give each child a sheet of black construction paper and a white crayon. Encourage him to use the crayon to draw an outdoor scene on the paper. Then provide fluorescent tempera paint in a shallow container. Invite each child to dip a fingertip into the paint and press several fingerprints onto the paper, to resemble fireflies flying in the air. When the paint dries, each child may add a head, legs, and wings to each firefly.

Mini Mooncakes

Invite youngsters to describe what the sky looks like at night. Ask them questions like "What does the moon look like? Have you seen several *phases* of the moon, such as *full, half-,* and *crescent* moons?" Draw a circle, a semicircle, and a crescent shape on the chalkboard to help students recall what they've seen.

Then bake some cupcakes for a yummy, hands-on experience with the shapes of the moon. Provide each child with an unfrosted, cooled, chocolate cupcake. Ask each child which moon shape she'd like her cupcake to resemble. If she wants to make a *full moon,* have her sprinkle powdered sugar over the whole top of the cupcake. If she'd like to make a *half-moon,* provide a tagboard semicircle cutout that covers half the cupcake top. Have her place the cutout on the cupcake and sprinkle powdered sugar on the uncovered section. If she'd like to make a *crescent moon,* provide her with a football-shaped cutout to place on her cupcake. Have her sprinkle powdered sugar on the uncovered section.

Invite youngsters to enjoy their cupcakes while you read *Mooncake* by Frank Asch (Simon And Schuster Books For Young Readers). Mmmmm!

A Celestial Ceiling

Stars add sparkle to the night sky. Share with your youngsters the traditional rhyme "Star Light, Star Bright." Then invite them to create their own wishing stars to brighten your classroom ceiling.

Duplicate the star pattern on page 64 on yellow construction paper for each child. Label one side of each star with a child's name. On the opposite side, write the child's dictation as he relates a wish. Have each child cut out his star. Then assist each child in squeezing glue around the edges of one side of his cutout. Have him sprinkle glitter or sequins on the glue, then shake off the excess. Allow the glue to dry. If desired, turn the star over and decorate the opposite side as well. Hang the finished stars from your classroom ceiling.

Ben

Sweet Dreams

Use stars and moons to invite sweet dreams when your little ones create painted pillowcases. Have each child bring a white or pastel-colored pillowcase from home. Purchase or cut several sponges in star and moon shapes. Working with one or two children at a time, insert a sheet of cardboard inside each pillowcase. Pour yellow, pink, and blue fabric paints into shallow containers. Encourage each youngster to press the sponges into the paint, then onto the side edges of her pillowcase. Let her watch as you use a squeeze bottle of fabric paint to write "Sweet Dreams For [Child's Name]" across the top of the pillowcase.

Allow the paint to dry thoroughly (at least overnight). Be sure to follow the instructions on the fabric-paint bottle to set the paint if necessary. If you are planning a class pajama party (see pages 60–61), have each child bring a pillow from home. Dress the pillows in the finished cases and use them during the festivities before sending them home.

Snuggle Up With A Good Book

Just Go To Bed
Written by Mercer Mayer
Published by Western Publishing
   Company, Inc.

Franklin In The Dark
Written by Paulette Bourgeois
Published by Scholastic Inc.

The Quilt
Written by Ann Jonas
Published by Greenwillow Books

Grandfather Twilight
Written by Barbara Berger
Published by Scholastic Inc.

Ten Flashing Fireflies
Written by Philemon Sturges
Published by North-South
   Books Inc.

When Sheep Cannot Sleep
Written by Satoshi Kitamura
Published by Farrar Straus
   Giroux

No Jumping On The Bed!
Written by Tedd Arnold
Published by Scholastic Inc.

It's PJ Day!

Get out those bunny slippers! It's time to finish up your nighttime theme with a Pajama Party Day. Ask a few parent volunteers to come in to help and join the fun. Night-night!

Getting Ready

Duplicate the invitation on page 64 and send it home with each child in your class. Then dress for the day yourself in pajamas, a robe, and the biggest, silliest slippers you can find! Set up five stations in your classroom for the five activities on these two pages. Ask your paraprofessional or parent volunteers to help you supervise the stations. Divide your class into five groups and let groups rotate to each of the stations throughout the party.

Station One—Bedtime Buddies

Invite students to gather all the bedtime buddies that class members have brought along for the day. Ask students to sort the stuffed animals and dolls by various attributes. Have them verbalize their reasoning as they work. Then ask children to compare the groups to determine more, fewer, and equal.

Station Two—Bedtime Snack

Read the story *Milk And Cookies* by Frank Asch (Parents Magazine Press). Then have youngsters enjoy a snack of milk and cookies in the classroom. Have the children use plastic knives to spread commercially prepared frosting on sugar cookies. Add colored sprinkles for a festive flair. Provide cold milk in paper cups and let little ones eat this nighttime treat!

Station Three—Counting Sheep

Since your pajama-clad pupils are probably nowhere close to sleepy, ask them to try counting some sheep. Bring out a bag of cotton balls (sheep, of course!) for some math practice. Number ten index cards with the numerals one through ten. Create a tabletop fence out of wooden blocks or LEGO® pieces. Then, as each child takes a turn, hold up a number card. Have the child make the designated number of sheep "jump" the fence as he counts aloud. Continue until all students have had a turn.

Station Four—A Bedtime Play

What do your students do at night when they can't sleep? Read aloud *Monster Can't Sleep* by Virginia Mueller (Albert Whitman & Company). Then have students relate the things they do or their parents do for them to help them fall asleep. Perhaps they have some creative excuses for not going to bed! Then ask students to tell you the reasons they need sleep. Guide them to responses such as the following: *to have energy to play, to be healthy, to be awake for learning at school,* etc. Then encourage youngsters to role-play. Assign the parts of parent and child to two volunteers. Ask the pair to pretend it's bedtime. What would each of them say? Repeat the role-playing until everyone has had a turn.

Goodnight spoon and goodnight moon.

To End The Party

After each group has visited all the stations, gather together and put your Pajama Party to rest. Read aloud the class book from Station Five as your bedtime story. Then let all your little ones settle in for a snooze with resting mats, sleeping bags, pillows, or blankets. Turn off the lights, close the blinds, and turn on a recording of lullabies. Tell your little ones that you're going to play the part of the sandman. Walk around the room and sprinkle sand (actually a small amount of clear glitter or talcum powder) on each of your little sleepyheads. (Be sure to keep the glitter or powder away from children's faces.) When it's time to arise from naptime, be sure to act out morning rituals. Set an alarm clock to buzz, turn on the lights, and open the blinds. Good morning, everyone! Did you sleep well?

Station Five—A Goodnight Book

Share the traditional bedtime story *Goodnight Moon* by Margaret Wise Brown (Harper & Row, Publishers, Inc.). After reading the story, point out the many rhyming words. Then have students contribute to a class book version of the story. Give each child a sheet of white art paper. Have her draw two items with rhyming names, such as *spoon* and *moon,* on the white paper and then cut them out. Have her glue the two cutouts to a sheet of green construction paper that has been programmed with "Goodnight _____ and goodnight _____," across the bottom. (The green paper represents "the great green room.") Print the two corresponding rhyming words in the blanks on each child's page. When all the groups have rotated through this station, bind the pages together with a cover that reads "Our Goodnight Book."

Time For Bed, Sleepyhead!

Dear Family,
We are learning about nighttime at school. Please talk with me about my bedtime. Show me what the clock looks like when it's my bedtime. Then help me fill in the blanks below.

When the big hand is on the _____

And the little hand is on the _____

It is _____.

It is bedtime!

This is what the clock's hands look like when it's my bedtime.

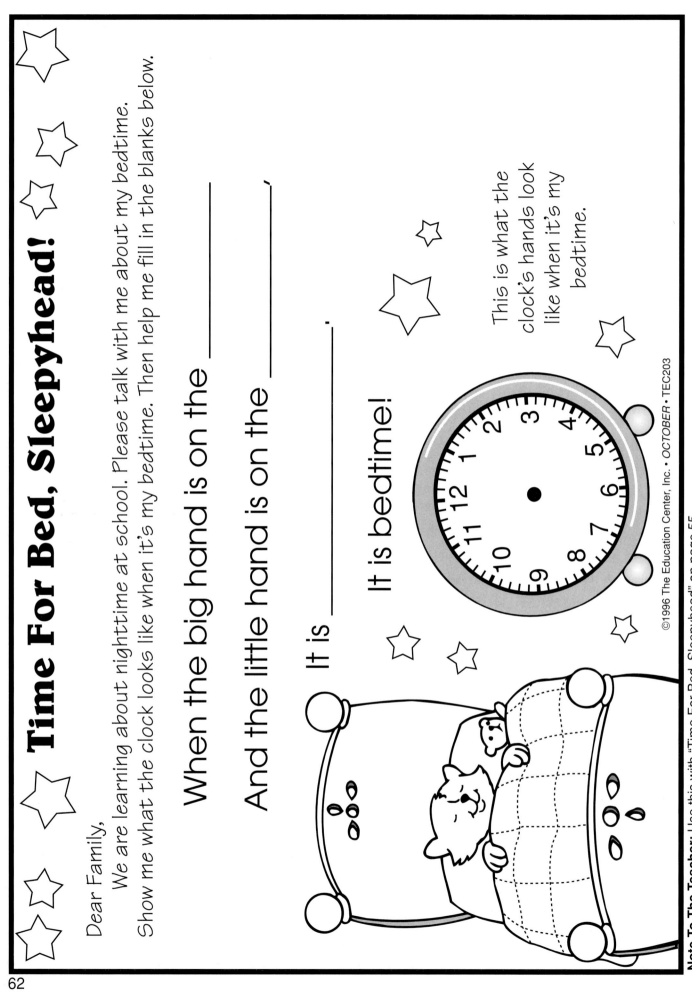

Note To The Teacher: Use this with "Time For Bed, Sleepyhead" on page 55.

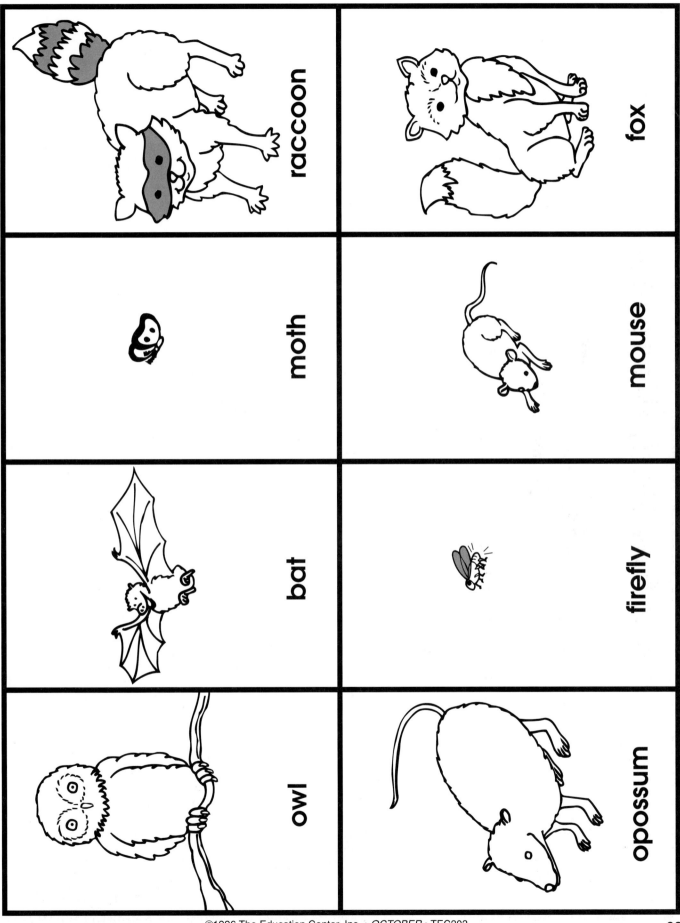

raccoon

fox

moth

mouse

bat

firefly

owl

opossum

Star Pattern
Use with "A Celestial Ceiling" on page 58.

Pajama-Party Day Invitation
Use with "Getting Ready" on page 60.

You're Invited To

Pajama Party Day!

We'll be having a special PJ Day at school on
_____. Please send your child to school
that day wearing pajamas or other sleepwear and comfort-
able shoes. (Have your child wear his or her jammies over
her regular clothing, if desired.) He or she should bring along
a favorite stuffed animal or other bedtime buddy. You may
also send in a comfy pillow, blanket, or sleeping bag.
Please let me know if *you* can join us, too!

Sweet dreams!

©1996 The Education Center, Inc. • *OCTOBER* • TEC203

MEET THE CORNFIELD CREW!

Take a trip to the cornfield to find a not-so-scary Mr. Scarecrow and his flying friends, a crop of corn-related activities, and a study of those corn-loving bandits—raccoons!

ideas by Lucia Kemp Henry

A Big Scarecrow Buddy

Create a lovable classroom scarecrow to capture students' interest and provide a focus for your cornfield activities. A few days before beginning your unit, collect a large supply of plastic grocery bags and some children's clothing—a sweatshirt or flannel shirt, pull-on pants or overalls, a pair of gardening gloves, and a pair of socks. To create the scarecrow's body, use the plastic bags to stuff the clothing. Use a few simple stitches with heavy-duty thread to sew the clothing together at strategic points, such as the waist and cuffs. Then insert a wire clothes hanger inside the shoulders of the stuffed shirt. Use pliers to pinch the hanger hook into a loop.

Fashion a head for the scarecrow by stuffing some plastic bags into a paper grocery bag. Gather the open end of the bag and secure it with a thick rubber band. Then slip the gathered end over the clothes-hanger loop. Hot-glue the head to the scarecrow's shirt collar. Also use hot glue to attach a child-sized straw hat. Paint a face on your scarecrow; then, if desired, add some finishing touches, such as suspenders or yarn hair.

When you're ready, introduce the scarecrow to your class. Invite the children to choose a name for him.

Doing Things With Mr. Scarecrow

Your scarecrow buddy is bound to be a popular addition to the classroom! Document his visit with a very special class book. Invite pairs or small groups of children to take turns posing for photos with Mr. Scarecrow as they go about their daily classroom activities. For instance, two or three children may want to take Mr. Scarecrow to the reading area to share a book. Or perhaps a pair of youngsters might let Mr. Scarecrow join them as they eat a snack. When you've snapped enough pictures to represent the activities of a typical school day, have the film developed. Place each picture in a photo album, along with a student-dictated caption describing each activity. This would be a perfect project to share with families during Parents' Night or Open House!

Anna and Li are reading books with Mr. Scarecrow.

A Not-So-Scary Scarecrow

Do your little ones understand the job of a scarecrow? Show students pictures (from nature magazines or nonfiction books) of a crow, a raccoon, a deer, a mouse, and a squirrel. Explain that these animals all like to eat corn and other crops. A farmer puts a scarecrow in his field, hoping the animals will think it is a real person and be frightened away.

Since their classroom scarecrow buddy is such a friendly sort, little ones may want to assure you that they aren't frightened of any old scarecrow! Teach them this poem to reflect those feelings:

> Scarecrow, Scarecrow,
> How scary can you be?
> You scared a [**crow**],
> But you didn't scare me!

Repeat the verse, replacing the boldfaced animal name with *raccoon, deer, mouse,* and *squirrel.* Can your youngsters think of more animal names to use in the poem?

A Scarecrow Booklet

Youngsters will love making these individual booklets that illustrate the poem in "A Not-So-Scary Scarecrow." For each child, duplicate the booklet pages on page 71 on white construction paper and the booklet backer on page 72 on tagboard or yellow cardstock. Cut out the face circle on each booklet backer. Position and glue a copy of a child's school photo behind the opening on his backer. Have each child write his name in the space provided and color the backer. Then have him color the animals on the first three booklet pages and draw an animal of his choice on the fourth page.

Fill in the blank with the child's dictation. If desired, provide each child with additional copies of the open page (white-out the page number before duplicating) so he can add more text and drawings to his booklet.

Assist each child with cutting the booklet pages apart and arranging them in numerical order (add page numbers to additional open pages as needed). Staple the pages to the booklet backer where indicated.

Singin' In The Cornfield

Teach your youngsters this song about a scarecrow's job. Encourage them to move each body part as it is named in the song.

A Scarecrow Song
(sung to the tune of "Daisy, Daisy,...")

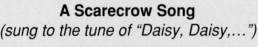

Mister Scarecrow,
Working so hard all day.
Mister Scarecrow,
Scaring the crows away!

You move your [arms] just so,
Until the crows must go.
Hooray, hooray!
You scared them away!
You're a scary old scarecrow!

Repeat the song several times—substituting other body parts, such as *hands, legs, feet,* and *head.*

Let's Be Raccoons!

A basket of fresh corn on the cob and some marvelous masks will have your little ones role-playing raccoons.

On the day of this activity, bring some unshucked corn to school. If you want students to role-play raccoons feasting on corn, prepare the masks in advance for younger students. For older children, make several tagboard copies of the mask pattern on page 73. Cut them out; then have each child use a mask template to trace the pattern onto black construction paper. Assist her in cutting out her mask, as well as two eyeholes. Poke a brad through each end of the mask and spread it open to secure it. Slip a thin rubber band around both brads to create an elastic band to fit each child's head.

Share Jim Arnosky's wonderful book, *Raccoons And Ripe Corn* (Lothrop, Lee, & Shepard Books). The evocative artwork in this Reading Rainbow selection puts you right in the middle of a field of ripe corn—along with a family of hungry raccoons! After reading the story, have youngsters recall the words that describe the raccoons' actions *(sneak, walk, climb, pull, peel, feast, eat, hurry)*. Then invite them to imitate some of these actions at their own corn feast!

Ask youngsters to help you peel the husks and silk strands from the corn and wash it. Enlist the help of your school cafeteria to cook the corn, or prepare it in the classroom using a Crock-Pot® or hot plate. (As always, use extra caution when using electrical appliances in the classroom.) Drain the cooked corn and let it cool until just warm. Provide butter and salt; then invite your little ones to wear their masks and role-play raccoons nibbling on the ripe corn. Have a camera handy—you'll want to record the antics of your corn-loving critters on film!

Cornfield Callers

Read *Raccoons* by K. M. Kostyal (National Geographic Society) to learn more about this frequent visitor to the cornfield. Then share the following facts about the rascally raccoon with your young learners:

- Raccoons are distinguished by the dark rings on their tails and the black masks on their faces.
- Raccoons have nimble fingers on their forepaws to help them find and eat many kinds of food.
- Raccoons are omnivorous. They eat fruits, vegetables, grain, insects, mice, birds, and frogs.
- Raccoons prefer to live in swampy areas or woods near water.
- Raccoons give birth to litters of one to seven babies, or cubs, at a time.
- Raccoons may frequent cornfields and often cause problems for farmers.

Paper-Plate Raccoons

Youngsters will enjoy creating these perky paper-plate raccoons using the patterns on pages 73 and 74. For each child, duplicate the patterns on page 73 on white construction paper and the ear-of-corn pattern on page 74 on yellow construction paper. Have each child color the mask and nose patterns black, and the ears, paws, and snout patterns brown. Help him cut out all the pieces and glue them to a thin white paper plate, as shown. Provide each child with two white paper reinforcers to stick to the mask pattern to resemble the raccoon's eyes. Then have him cut out the ear-of-corn pattern and glue it to the raccoon's paws. Save the finished raccoons to add to the bulletin board described in "A Delightfully Corny Crop" on page 70.

Hello, Crow!

Another frequent visitor to the cornfield is the crow. Show your youngsters a picture of a crow from a nature magazine or nonfiction book. Explain that crows can be both helpful and pesky to the farmer. Crows eat insects that can destroy a farmer's crops—that's good. But crows also like to eat the sprouting corn—that's bad! Teach your little ones this verse about some crows who like to visit Old MacDonald's cornfield.

Two little crows,
All dressed in black—
One named Jimmy,
The other one, Jack.

All day long,
The corn they'd eat
In Old MacDonald's
Field so neat.

They ate that corn
Until one day,
Mac got a scarecrow
And shooed them away!

There went Jimmy!
There went Jack!
They flew right off
And never came back!
—Ada Hamrick

Something To Crow About

These crows will "caws" your youngsters to display their artistic skills! Duplicate the crow pattern on page 74 on white construction paper for each child. Have each child cut out his pattern. Assist him in using pieces of rolled masking tape to attach the crow cutout to a sheet of newspaper. Encourage each youngster to use black and blue tempera paint to sponge-paint his cutout. Allow the paint to dry; then provide each child with two white paper reinforcers to represent the crow's eyes. If desired, have him glue several black craft feathers to the crow's wings and tail. Have each child glue a yellow construction-paper beak to his crow. Save the finished raccows to display on the bulletin board described in "A Delightfully Corny Crop" on page 70.

Johnnycakes

(makes about 12 servings)

1 egg, beaten
2 cups ground cornmeal
1 Tbsp. sugar
1 tsp. salt
1 1/4–1 1/2 cups milk

Stir all the ingredients together in a large bowl. Drop spoonfuls of batter into a hot, well-greased electric frying pan. Fry to a golden brown on both sides. Stir the remaining batter occasionally to keep it well mixed. Serve the cakes warm with butter.

Totally Tasty Corn Cakes

If your youngsters tasted ripe corn on the cob with the activity "Let's Be Raccoons!" on page 67, you've already established that raccoons and crows aren't the only ones who like to eat corn! People the world over consider corn an important food staple. Have students help you cook up a corny treat to explore one of the many ways corn can be eaten. First read the classic Caldecott Honor Book, *Journey Cake, Ho!* by Ruth Sawyer (Puffin Books). Then prepare a batch of old-timey johnnycakes.

The Corn Taste Test

Your youngsters may be amazed at how many common American foods are made from corn. Bring in a variety of corn-based foods to conduct a classroom taste test. Include a corn-based cereal (such as Corn Chex® or Kix®), corn chips, corn tortillas, popcorn, and canned whole-kernel corn. Display all the foods and discuss with students which ones they have tasted before. Invite each child to taste a sample of each type of food and determine a favorite. Create a class graph to display the results.

Delicious Dishes

Follow up your taste test by having each child illustrate her favorite corn-based food on a sheet of white drawing paper. Cut around each child's drawing; then glue it to a sheet of colored construction paper. Have the child explain why she favors that particular corn dish. Write her dictation below her picture. Staple the completed pages together between construction-paper covers. Print the title "Delicious Corn Dishes" on the front cover. Invite students to cut pictures of corn-based foods from magazines to glue onto the book's cover. Add the book to your classroom library.

Josie likes popcorn because it's crunchy.

69

Corny Collages

Encourage your little ones to be creative with these corn collages. For each child, duplicate two copies of the ear-of-corn pattern on page 74 on white or yellow construction paper. Have each child cut out her patterns. Then provide glue and a variety of collage materials, such as squares cut from construction paper, magazine paper, crepe paper, or bulletin-board border; popped popcorn; Styrofoam® packing peanuts; small pom-poms; or cereal pieces. For inspiration, place a few ears of fresh sweet corn and some decorative Indian corn on the tabletop where children are working. Ask each child to select her own combination of materials to glue onto her cutouts. When the corn projects have dried, have each child glue a green construction-paper husk to one of the cutouts. Print the child's name on the husk. Use this personalized ear of corn as a cubby marker, center marker, or place card for a class party. Display the remaining ears of corn on the bulletin board described in "A Delightfully Corny Crop."

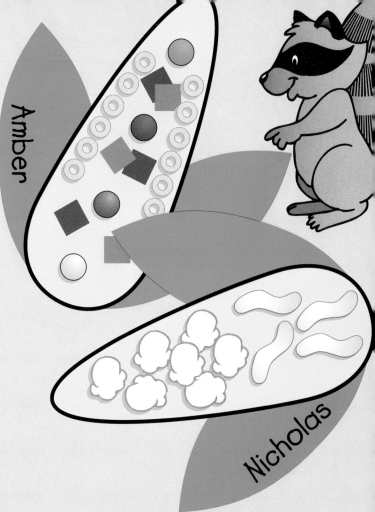

A Delightfully Corny Crop

Cultivate a classroom cornfield when you create this bulletin-board display! Cover the board with light blue paper to resemble sky. Add a strip of brown paper across the bottom to represent soil. Use your scarecrow buddy (described in "A Big Scarecrow Buddy" on page 65) as a centerpiece for the display. Attach him to the board with pushpins at the edges of his clothing—or prop him up on a table pushed under the board or to one side of it. Next cut strips of green bulletin-board paper in varying lengths. Staple the strips along the bottom of the bulletin board to resemble cornstalks. To each cornstalk, attach several of the students' corn projects from "Corny Collages." Add green crepe-paper husks to each ear of corn. Tuck a few thin strips of yellow construction paper or some strands of yellow, plastic Easter grass behind the tip of each ear of corn to resemble corn silk. Add the student-made raccoons and crows from "Paper-Plate Raccoons" and "Something To Crow About" on page 68. Your cornfield is complete!

You scared a crow.

1

You scared a raccoon.

2

You scared a deer.

3

You scared a _____.

4

Booklet Backer

Use with "A Scarecrow Booklet" on page 66.

But you didn't scare me!

Cut out.

Staple little booklet pages here.

Scarecrow, Scarecrow,
How scary can you be?

This book was made by _____

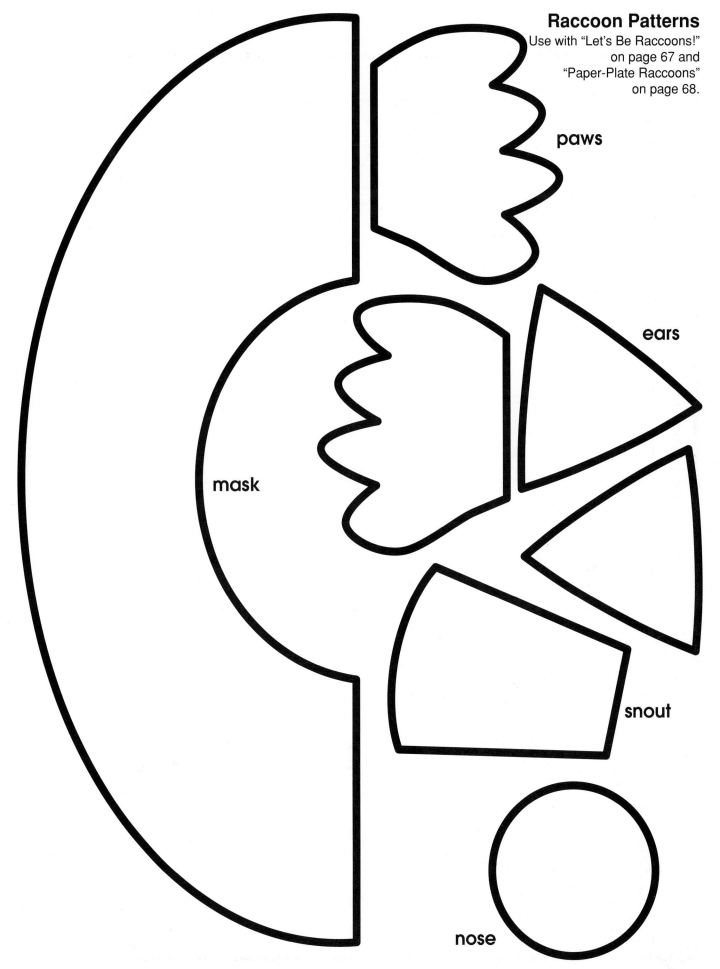

Raccoon Patterns
Use with "Let's Be Raccoons!"
on page 67 and
"Paper-Plate Raccoons"
on page 68.

paws

ears

mask

snout

nose

Ear-Of-Corn Pattern

Use with "Paper-Plate Raccoons" on page 68 and "Corny Collages" on page 70.

Crow Pattern

Use with "Something To Crow About" on page 68.

Project PUMPKIN

Convert your classroom into a pumpkin paradise; then provide lots of opportunities for your young P.I.'s—Pumpkin Investigators—to explore and experience pumpkins!

ideas contributed by Lucia Kemp Henry

Pumpkin Paradise

Before beginning your investigation of pumpkins, create a pumpkin paradise that even the most hard-nosed detective can't resist. During a visit to a pumpkin patch or farmers' market, have students select lots of different sizes, shapes, and shades of pumpkins to bring back to class. If a trip cannot be arranged, request that parents send pumpkins to school. Place the pumpkins all around the room in conspicuous and accessible locations.

Decorate your doorway in grand pumpkin style to invite young inspectors into the pumpkin paradise. Cut two lengths of bulletin-board paper several feet longer than the height of your classroom doorway. Also cut a length of paper the width of the doorway. Have students sponge-paint each length of paper with various shades of orange tempera paint. When the paint is dry, tape the long sheets of paper along each side of the door frame and the short sheet over the top. Using a marker, draw the outline of a pumpkin on the paper around the door. Loosen the outer edges of the paper to cut along the outline. After cutting, tape the outer edges of the pumpkin to the wall. If desired, embellish the pumpkin with a stem and green, twisted-paper vines and leaves. What a perfect entry into a pumpkin paradise!

What's Inside?

Orange, odd-shaped, and oh-so-big may be how a pumpkin appears on the outside, but what's inside? Pose this question to your student detectives. Then invite several volunteers to select pumpkins to be cut open. Using a large knife, cut the pumpkins in half vertically from stem to bottom. Have children inspect and describe the cross sections of the pumpkins—the thick flesh, the thin skin, the stringy fibers in the pulp, and the seeds. Find out if students know which part is used in pumpkin pie. Then preserve some key elements of the pumpkins for use in future investigations. Have children help scoop out the pulp and seeds. Rinse the seeds well, spread them on newspaper, and set them aside to dry overnight. Use the seeds later in "The Story Of A Pumpkin Seed," "What Do Pumpkins Need To Grow?", and "Listen And Count" on page 77. Keep the pumpkin halves and a few seeds to use in "Hide-And-Seek Pumpkin Pal" on page 80.

The Investigation Continues

To continue sharpening their investigative skills, encourage your little inspectors to examine the many external characteristics of pumpkins. First read or para-phrase *The Pumpkin Patch* by Elizabeth King (Dutton Children's Books). Then, in each of several centers, arrange three distinctly different-sized pumpkins on separate sheets of chart paper. If desired, provide a magnifying glass in each center. Invite small groups of students to closely inspect—by looking at, touching, and holding—the pumpkins in their centers. Ask them to describe each pumpkin based on their investigations of its size, color, texture, shape, and weight. Record the descriptions on the chart paper under each pumpkin. Conclude the investigations with a review of the lists from each center. Follow up this activity by presenting each child with the award on page 84.

big
heavy
orange

Our Pumpkin Book

From the information gathered in "What's Inside?" on page 75 and "The Investigation Continues," your Pumpkin Investigators can draw their own conclusions about the characteristics of pumpkins. Then they can draw their own pumpkin pictures for this puffy pumpkin big book!

Obtain two same-sized pizza rounds to use as covers for the book. Using one pizza round, cut a classroom quantity of circles from large sheets of white construction paper for the book's pages. Then cut a piece of orange fabric one inch larger than the pizza round. Wrap the fabric over the edge of the pizza round and hot-glue it in place around all but a small section, pleating as neces-sary to make it fit. Lightly stuff fiberfill into the opening. Then finish gluing the fabric to the pizza round to seal the opening. Glue a short tagboard stem on the back of the pumpkin. Use a laundry marker or fabric paint to write the title "Our Pumpkin Book" on the finished cover. With orange tempera paint, sponge-paint the other pizza round to use as the back book cover.

Have each child illustrate the inside or outside of a pumpkin on a white construction-paper circle. Encourage him to write or dictate one or two descriptive sentences about his pumpkin. Assemble the pages between the covers. At the top on each side of the pumpkin stem, make holes in both covers and each page. Fasten metal rings through the holes to make a big flip book. Encour-age youngsters to share the book with partners, making inquiries about one another's pumpkin pictures.

Our
Pumpkin
Book

My pumpkin is bumpy. –Patrick

What Do Pumpkins Need To Grow?

Encourage your little sleuths to dig into a book full of clues to discover what pumpkins need to flourish. Before revealing the book, prepare a large tray of soil, a partially filled watering can, and a container of pumpkin seeds. To represent the sun, place a flashlight with the other items. Then read *It's Pumpkin Time!* by Zoe Hall (The Blue Sky Press). Afterward discuss the growth needs of a pumpkin—soil, sun, and water or rain. In turn, have each student demonstrate her understanding of what is needed to grow a pumpkin. Encourage her to bury a seed in the soil, then give it water from the watering can and sunlight from the flashlight. It's elementary! Pumpkins have very simple needs.

The Story Of A Pumpkin Seed

Have young detectives track the growth of a pumpkin seed by making these individual booklets. For each child, duplicate pages 81 and 82. Cut the booklet pages apart. Guide the children to complete each page as described, using the dried pumpkin seeds from "What's Inside?" on page 75 as needed. When finished, sequence the pages and staple them along the left side. Encourage each student to share her booklet with a partner—and later, with family members at home.

- **Cover:** Color the mouse. Glue a pumpkin seed over the seed in the mouse's paws.
- **Page 1:** Draw and color a pumpkin on the seed packet. Glue a few seeds near the packet opening.
- **Page 2:** Sponge-paint brown soil beneath the dotted line. Glue a seed to the X.
- **Page 3:** Glue two leaf cutouts to the stem. Draw rain. Glue a seed to the X.
- **Page 4:** Draw a sun in the top left corner. Color the leaves and blossoms.
- **Page 5:** Use cotton swabs dipped in orange paint to color the pumpkin.

Listen And Count

Advise your investigators to perk up their ears for this counting game! To prepare, duplicate, color, and cut out the pumpkin-seed patterns on page 84. Glue each pattern to a separate square of tagboard; then laminate the cards for durability. Place a tray of dry pumpkin seeds (saved from "What's Inside?" on page 75), the facedown stack of cards, and an open-topped plastic pumpkin on the floor. To play, have the children turn their backs to the pumpkin. Invite one child to turn around and select a card from the top of the stack, then take that number of seeds from the tray. Have him slowly drop one seed at a time into the pumpkin. Encourage the other students to listen and count the number of seeds they hear being dropped. Then have them turn around and tell the number of seeds they think were put in the pumpkin. Ask the child who selected the number card to show it to the others, so that they can check their responses. Remove the seeds from the pumpkin and count them together. Continue play, following the same procedures to give each child a turn. *Plink, plink, plink.* Count on these clues to arrive at your conclusion!

A House For A Mouse

Detectives know that when someone wants to hide evidence, he often discards it. Perhaps the owner of the jack-o'-lantern in *Mousekin's Golden House* by Edna Miller (Prentice-Hall, Inc.) had nothing to hide, but his discarded treasure had lots to offer a curious mouse. Prior to reading the story, prepare the puppet on page 83. First duplicate the patterns on page 84 for later use. Then glue page 83 to a piece of tagboard. Cut out the jack-o'-lantern and mouse patterns; then laminate them for durability. Cut a slit along the dotted line near the top of the jack-o'-lantern. To create a back for the puppet, trace around the jack-o'-lantern on a piece of orange felt. Cut the felt along the outline. Hot-glue one end of a length of green ribbon—the vine—to the stem of the felt cutout. Then hot-glue the jack-o'-lantern to the felt along the side and top edges. Attach the mouse to the other end of the ribbon. To use the puppet, simply slide one hand into the opening of the jack-o'-lantern and move the mouse with the other hand. Following a reading of the story, have students take turns using the puppet with this rhyme.

Little mouse, little mouse,
Would you like a pumpkin house?
How will you get in?

Look all around.	*(Circle the mouse around the pumpkin.)*
Jump up and down.	*(Move the mouse up and down.)*
Climb up the side.	*(Move the mouse up one side.)*
Crawl behind and hide!	*(Hide the mouse behind the pumpkin.)*
Dance on the top.	*(Make the mouse dance on top of the pumpkin.)*
Look down and stop!	*(Make the mouse freeze in place.)*
Squeeze your body in.	*(Push the mouse through the slit.)*
You've found a home again!	*(Use the hand inside the puppet to turn the mouse so that it peeks out through the slit.)*

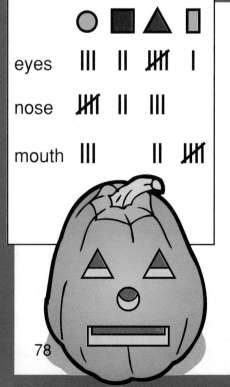

Jack-O'-Lantern Time!

Even inexperienced detectives will gather that—with all the pumpkins lying around—a jack-o'-lantern carving is sure to occur! So set out in search of the perfect pumpkin from your pumpkin paradise and get ready to carve. But first have youngsters use the democratic process to decide on the shapes they want used in creating their jack-o'-lantern. Across the top of a sheet of chart paper, draw a circle, square, triangle, and rectangle. Down the left side of the sheet, write the words "eyes," "nose," and "mouth." As a group, have students vote on the shape they prefer to use for each of the features of the jack-o'-lantern. Record the number of votes for each shape and feature with tally marks. Then draw and cut the jack-o'-lantern's features according to the greatest number of votes for each. Save the pumpkin cutouts to use in "A Taste Of Pumpkin" on page 79.

Enjoy the jack-o'-lantern in class for a while; then set it outdoors. Ask students to predict what will happen to the jack-o'-lantern. Then visit it often to observe its fate.

A Taste Of Pumpkin

Invite your supersleuths to taste pumpkin that has been prepared in a variety of ways. In advance cut small pieces of raw pumpkin (use the cutouts from "Jack-O'-Lantern Time!" on page 78). Boil or bake some of the pieces until they are tender. Then warm up pumpkin from a can. Serve children a small amount of each type of pumpkin. Ask them to describe each flavor and texture. Find out if students have a preference for one kind of pumpkin over another. Record their preferences on a graph; then determine which kind of pumpkin is most favored by the class.

Petite Pumpkin Pies

These personal pumpkin pies will be the perfect treat for your busy little investigators! Purchase enough canned pumpkin-pie filling and individual pastry shells to make one pie per student. Following the recipe on the cans, have students help prepare the pie filling. Encourage them to count the spoonfuls of filling needed for each pie. Bake the pies for 15 minutes in a 425° oven. Then reduce the oven temperature to 350° and bake the pies for approximately 40 minutes. When the pies are cool, serve one to each child. As they indulge, have students discuss the look of the pie filling before and after baking. Ask them to describe the smell of the pies; then tell what makes the pies smell that way. Find out if students like the pies. As they give their responses, make tallies under the appropriate yes or no column on a sheet of chart paper. Count the number of tallies for each response. As a class, compare the numbers to determine if more students liked or did not like the pumpkin pies.

How Much Do I Love Pumpkin Pie?

Whether the petite pumpkin pies suited their tastes or not, little detectives will certainly enjoy the opportunity to act out this rhyming inquisition.

How much do I love pumpkin pie?
As much as bluebirds love the sky!   *(Flap arms like a flying bird.)*
As much as kitty cats love cream.   *(Purr like a kitten.)*
As much as babies like to dream.   *(Lay head on folded hands and pretend to sleep.)*

How much do I love pumpkin pie?
As much as french fries love to fry!   *(Make a sizzling sound.)*
As much as piggies love the mud.   *(Make a grunting sound.)*
As much as buddies love their "bud."   *(Put arm around neighbor's shoulder.)*

How much do I love pumpkin pie?
As much as kids love asking, "Why?"   *(Extend hands with palms upward and arms bent.)*
As much as froggies love to hop.   *(Hop on floor like a frog.)*
As much as popcorn loves to pop.   *(Jump up and down in place.)*

How much do I love pumpkin pie?
I **really** love it. My, oh, my!   *(Rub tummy and smile.)*

—Lucia Kemp Henry

Hide-And-Seek Pumpkin Pal

Your Pumpkin Investigators will enjoy playing a game of hide-and-seek with this little mouse pumpkin pal. To make a mouse, glue two pumpkin-seed ears and two wiggle eyes onto a large pom-pom. Add a short length of yarn for the tail. With the flat sides down, place four or more pumpkin halves from "What's Inside?" (page 75) in a row on the floor. Have students observe as you hide the mouse under one of the pumpkin halves. Explain that each child will have a turn to find the mouse. To play with younger children, invite a volunteer to circle around the pumpkins as you sing "Where Is Little Mouse?" below. At the end of the song, ask him to lift the pumpkin he thinks the mouse is hiding under. If his first choice is incorrect, encourage him to continue his search for the mouse using deductive reasoning. To challenge an older child, encourage him to watch as the pumpkins are randomly rearranged during his turn. Then have him guess which pumpkin the mouse is under. Continue play to give every student a turn to find the mouse.

Where Is Little Mouse?

(sung to the tune of "Paw Paw Patch")

Where, oh where, is Little Mouse hiding?
Where, oh where, is Little Mouse hiding?
Where, oh where, is Little Mouse hiding?
He's hiding under a pumpkin shell!

Storytime Snack

Before wrapping up Project PUMPKIN, have youngsters use this simple mixture to sculpt a pumpkin-shaped snack. For ten servings, mix three cups of miniature marshmallows and one-quarter cup of margarine in a large saucepan. Warm the mixture over low heat until the marshmallows melt. To tint the mixture orange, stir in a few drops of red and yellow food coloring. Gradually fold in five cups of Apple Cinnamon CheeriOs®. Lightly coat each child's fingers with vegetable oil cooking spray. When the mixture has cooled sufficiently, give each child one-half cup of the mixture to form into a pumpkin shape. Have him press a green gumdrop on top of his pumpkin to represent the stem. Set the pumpkin snacks aside on waxed paper until they are firm. To conclude your class pumpkin investigations, serve the treats to youngsters during the reading of a pumpkin-related story.

Pumpkin Books Worth Investigating

Pumpkin Pumpkin
Written by Jeanne Titherington
Published by Greenwillow Books

The Biggest Pumpkin Ever
Written by Steven Kroll
Published by Holiday House, Inc.

Growing Pumpkins
Written by Melvin Berger
Published by Newbridge Communications, Inc.

The Story Of A Pumpkin Seed

Pumpkin Seeds

A little mouse plants
A tiny pumpkin seed.
Will the seed grow?
What will it need?

1

The seed needs the **soil**
To keep it warm and snug,
To keep it very safe
From a snail or a bug!

X

2

The seed needs the **rain**
To help it sprout and grow.
It grows a bit each day
'Til it has leaves, you know.

X

3

The plant needs the **sun**
For leaves and blossoms, too.
A tiny pumpkin needs sunshine
To grow bigger, just like you!

4

Soil and rain and sunshine
Make the pumpkin grow each day.
And soon the tiny pumpkin
Has grown up all the way!

5

Pumpkin-Seed Patterns Use with "Listen And Count" on page 77.

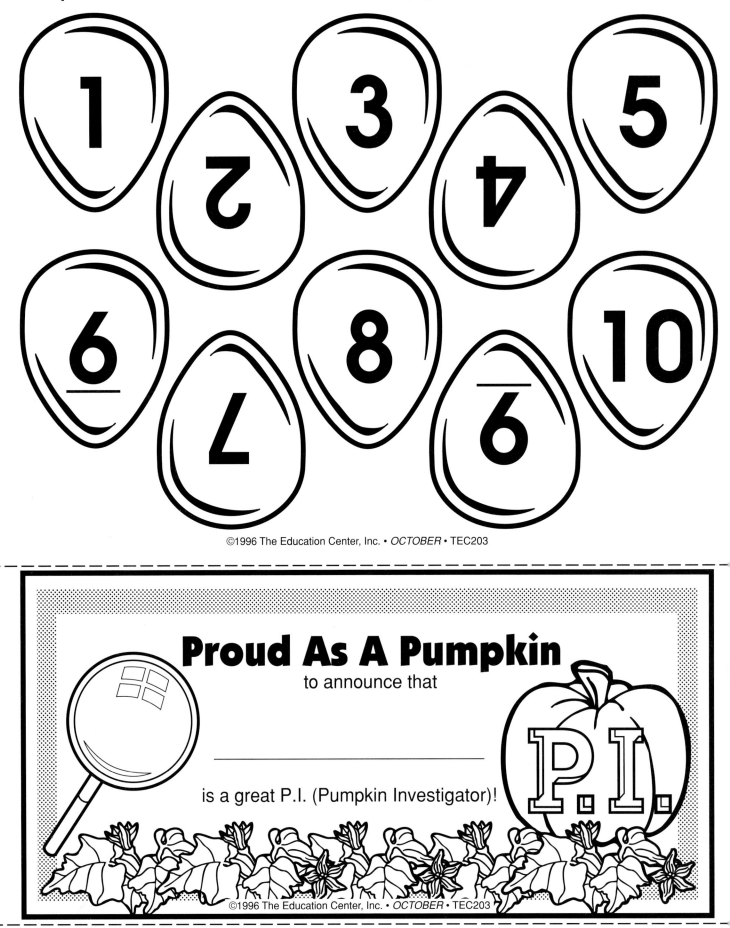

1 2 3 4 5 6 7 8 9 10

©1996 The Education Center, Inc. • *OCTOBER* • TEC203

Proud As A Pumpkin

to announce that

_____

is a great P.I. (Pumpkin Investigator)!

P.I.

©1996 The Education Center, Inc. • *OCTOBER* • TEC203

Note To The Teacher: For each child, duplicate and personalize the award before sending it home.

IT'S TRICK-OR-TREAT TIME!

It's time for cool costumes, pretty pumpkins, spooky stories, and tasty treats! Have some fun with these Halloween activities, including some ideas for a "spook-tacular" classroom celebration!

ideas contributed by Janet Czapla and Ada Hamrick

WHAT IS HALLOWEEN?

Even your youngest trick-or-treaters are probably familiar with some of the traditions of Halloween. Review the fun aspects of the holiday with a reading of Harriet Ziefert's *What Is Halloween?* (HarperCollins Publishers). Then teach little ones this Halloween poem:

HALLOWEEN IS...

Halloween is cats and bats
And jack-o'-lanterns bright.
Halloween is dressing up
To trick-or-treat at night.

Halloween is candy corn
And haunted houses, too.
Halloween is spooky stuff
And fun for me and you!

HALLOWEEN FEELINGS

Children may experience many different emotions related to Halloween. Encourage your youngsters to share stories about their Halloween experiences. Guide them to discuss events that made them feel happy, surprised, excited, apprehensive, or scared. In particular, talk about the difference between being scared in a fun way and being scared in a serious way. Then give students an opportunity to illustrate various types of feelings.

First add some red and yellow food coloring to a large bottle of white shampoo or milk bath. Pour one-half cup of the resulting orange liquid into a zippered plastic sandwich bag for each child. Squeeze as much air as possible out of the bag; then use masking tape to seal the top to prevent leakage. Have each child place his plastic bag flat on a tabletop. Then describe a Halloween situation to the students, such as "Your friend is wearing a monster mask." Invite each child to use his finger to "draw" a face on the bag that displays his emotional reaction to the situation described. When everyone has finished, have the children smooth away their drawings. Repeat the activity with other descriptions.

85

GLOWING JACK

Your youngsters' faces will light up when you use this jolly jack-o'-lantern puppet—and so will his! Begin by sponge-painting a paper lunch bag with orange tempera paint. When the paint is dry, turn the bag so that the bottom of the bag serves as the top of the jack-o'-lantern. Cut out eyes, a nose, and a mouth from one side of the bag. Gather the open end of the bag around the light end of a standard flashlight; then secure it with a rubber band. The flashlight will serve as the puppet's handle. Make your jack-o'-lantern glow by turning on the flashlight. Dim the classroom lights; then have each youngster, in turn, operate the Glowing Jack as classmates recite this poem. Invite the child holding the jack-o'-lantern puppet to shout "Boo!" at the end of the rhyme.

Mr. Jack-O'-Lantern,
How do you do?
Turn on your light
And then say, "Boo!"

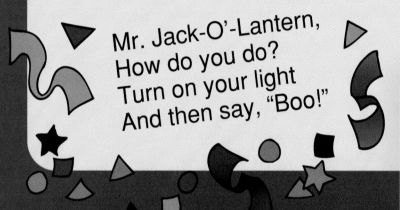

JACK SAYS

Play a Halloween version of the traditional Simon Says game to get your little ones moving. If you made the jack-o'-lantern puppet described in "Glowing Jack," use it for this activity. Adjust your classroom lights low enough for the flashlight's glow to be easily seen. Turn the flashlight on when you wish youngsters to begin a movement; then turn it off to signal them to stop.

To play Jack Says, give the players simple directions based on Halloween characters, such as "fly like a bat," "hoot like an owl," or "dance like a ballerina." Then give each youngster a turn to manipulate the puppet and call out a command for the game.

JACK-O-LOOPS

This group project will result in a festive decoration for a bulletin board. In advance cut a supply of 3" x 12" strips of orange construction paper and 2" x 12" strips of black construction paper. Invite each child to create a jack-o'-lantern face in the center of an orange strip using markers, crayons, or black construction-paper scraps and glue. Roll the finished strip into a loop and staple the ends together. The result—a jack-o-loop! If desired, have each child create more than one jack-o-loop. Then form the jack-o-loops into a paper chain. Place two jack-o-loops side by side, so that both faces are toward you. Thread a black strip through the two jack-o-loops and staple the ends of the strip together. Continue in this fashion until all the jack-o-loops are connected. Display the finished chain as a border on a Halloween bulletin board.

A HAUNTED NEIGHBORHOOD

Get your youngsters in the Halloween spirit with this ghostly bulletin-board design. Begin by creating a large supply of lima-bean ghosts. Purchase some large, dried lima beans. On each bean, use a permanent marker to draw a simple ghost's face. Then duplicate the haunted-house pattern on page 92 on white construction paper for each child. Have each child color his house pattern, then cut it out. Give each youngster a few lima-bean ghosts to glue onto his house. After the glue dries, mount all the houses on a bulletin board covered with black or dark blue paper. Have the youngsters help you add some spooky touches to the display, such as twisted crepe-paper trees and silver star stickers in the sky. Use the paper-chain border from "Jack-O-Loops" on page 86 to add a festive finish to this "boo-tiful" board!

SHADOW PUPPETS

For more haunted-house fun, set up a shadow center in your classroom. First duplicate the shadow-puppet patterns on page 94 on construction paper. Laminate and cut out the patterns; then tape each one to the end of a different craft stick. Use an opaque projector to enlarge the haunted-house pattern on page 92 on a length of white or yellow bulletin-board paper. Add details around the house such as a moon and stars or a picket fence. Then tape the paper to a low area of a classroom wall. Set up a filmstrip projector to shine light on the scene. Show the students how to hold the puppets between the light and the wall scene to create shadows. Encourage students to use the puppets and the haunted-house setting to dramatize Halloween stories. What little one could resist this spooky center?

GUESS WHO

"What are you going to be for Halloween?" That's a popular question at this time of year! Create a lift-the-flap class book to give each youngster a chance to reveal his choice of costume. First gather pictures of children's Halloween or career-related costumes from sources such as newspaper sales flyers, gift catalogs, or school-supply catalogs. To prepare pages for the book, program a sheet of copy paper with the open sentence, "Guess who wants to be a _____." Duplicate the programmed page on a sheet of construction paper for each child. Then glue a photocopy of a different child's school photo to the center of each page, and write that child's name below his photo.

Invite each child to choose a picture of a costume he likes. Have him glue the picture to a half-sheet of construction paper. Assist him in stapling the half-sheet of paper over the school photo on his book page. Fill in the blank with his dictation. Bind the students' pages between construction-paper covers. Read the book to the class, lifting the pictures to reveal each child's identity.

Then follow up with dress-up fun! Collect a variety of hats, masks, clothing, and props for your dramatic play area. Have a mirror handy so students can admire themselves in cool costumes of their own creation!

Guess who wants to be a <u>firefighter</u>.

Amy wants to be a <u>firefighter</u>.

MIRROR PAINTING

For more delightful disguises, try this neat twist on face painting. In advance collect a few large hand mirrors. Then pour a few colors of tempera paint into shallow pans. Add a small amount of dishwashing liquid to each pan. Then, working with one small group at a time, give each child a mirror. Invite him to look at his reflection. Then have him finger-paint features onto the surface of the mirror to alter his reflection. Offer suggestions for additions such as glasses, freckles, wild hair, hats, or mustaches. When finished, rinse and dry the mirrors; then invite the next small group to mirror-paint. You'll hear giggles galore as your little ones design their disguises!

SCARE UP A STORY!

Share these Halloween tales with your little boys and ghouls!

FIVE LITTLE PUMPKINS

Illustrated by Iris Van Rynbach
(Boyds Mills Press, Inc.)

Youngsters will love the bright, happy illustrations in this version of the traditional fingerplay. After reading the book and performing the fingerplay together, invite students to create their own illustrations to accompany the rhyme. Provide each child with a sheet of black construction paper, a handful of craft sticks, and five circles cut from orange construction paper. Have each child glue his craft sticks side by side along the bottom of the paper to resemble a wooden gate. Then have him draw a jack-o'-lantern face on each of the orange circles. Ask him to glue the five jack-o'-lanterns side by side along the top of the gate. Have him add stems to the pumpkins and stars to the sky using construction-paper scraps. Display the finished projects on a wall or bulletin board, along with a copy of the fingerplay printed on a sheet of chart paper.

MORE SPOOKY STORIES

Trick Or Treat, Little Critter®
By Gina and Mercer Mayer
Western Publishing Company, Inc.

Big Pumpkin
By Erica Silverman
Scholastic Inc.

The Hallo-Wiener
By Dav Pilkey
Scholastic Inc.

Trick Or Treat, Danny!
By Edith Kunhardt
Greenwillow Books

HARRIET'S HALLOWEEN CANDY

by Nancy Carlson
(Carolrhoda Books, Inc.)

Harriet learns the value of sharing when she experiences a candy overload at Halloween. Before eating her candy, Harriet organizes it by color, size, and favorite kind. Involve your youngsters in some Halloween candy classification of their own. Ask a few parents to donate bags of wrapped candies. Mix up the different kinds of candies in a large container. Have small groups of children sort the candies by various criteria, such as color, brand logo, size, or shape. Invite each youngster to select a treat to enjoy. Save the remainder of the candy to use with "Trick-Or-Treat Game" on page 90.

TUNES TO TRICK-OR-TREAT BY!

"Looking For Dracula"
Sung by Charlotte Diamond
10 Carrot Diamond; Hug Bug Music Inc.
To order, call Educational Record Center
1-800-438-1637.

"Everybody Freeze"
Sung by Joe Scruggs
Abracadabra; Shadow Play Records
To order, call 1-800-274-8804.

"As Scared As I Can Be"
Sung by Mr. Al
Mr. Al Sings Friends And Feelings;
Melody House
To order, call 1-800-234-9228.

89

A "SPOOK-TACULAR" CELEBRATION!

How about a festive finale for your Halloween happenings? Invite some parent volunteers to help out with some small-group activities. Then have everyone join together for some fun and games to end this ghoulish gala!

TRICK-OR-TREAT GAME

Little ones will love this tasty game so much, they won't even notice that they're practicing taking turns, sharing, and counting. In advance fill a plastic pumpkin with wrapped candies. (If desired, use the candy from *Harriet's Halloween Candy* on page 89.) Prepare the playing cards on pages 93 and 95 after duplicating pages 94 and 96 for later use. Glue pages 93 and 95 to sheets of tagboard. Cut the cards apart; then laminate them for durability.

Play this game in small groups. Place the cards facedown in a pile. In turn, have each player choose a card. Ask an adult volunteer to read the instructions on the card. If it is a "Trick" card, have the child lead the group in performing the trick. If it is a "Treat" card, ask the child to count out the designated number of treats from the plastic pumpkin. If it is a "Share" card, encourage the player to share one or more of his treats with another player. If a child draws a "Share" card when he has no treats, place the card on the bottom of the pile and have him draw again. When the pile of cards is depleted, mix up the cards and begin again!

A MEAL FIT FOR A MONSTER

Your little monsters will be "goblin" this terrifying treat!

Monster Mash
(serves 1)

1 scoop Boo Goo (vanilla ice cream)
1 Tbsp. Swamp Mud (chocolate syrup)
1 Tbsp. Spider Fangs (miniature chocolate chips)
10 Mummy Toes (miniature marshmallows)

Place the ingredients in a paper cup. Mash them together with a plastic spoon. Top with a spoonful of Snake Slime (green-tinted whipped cream). Devour it if you dare!

BOO BREW

Your youngsters will be stir-crazy over this classification activity! In advance draw a large kettle shape on a piece of black bulletin-board paper. Cut it out and glue it to a large cardboard box. Borrow an oversized spoon or paddle from your school cafeteria and you'll be ready to make Boo Brew. Have each child in a small group search the room for the ingredients for your brew by giving instructions such as, "Bring something red," or "Bring something that starts with the *S* sound." As each child places his item in the imaginary pot, give him a turn to stir the brew with the spoon or paddle. After everyone has contributed, gather the children around the pot to take an imaginary sip of the mixture. Encourage the students to register their reaction with a loud "Boo-oooo!" Then start over with a new brew!

A ROLLICKING RELAY

Draw jack-o'-lantern faces on a few miniature gourds. Then use the gourds for this relay race. Divide the class into teams of three or four. Have each team line up one child behind another on one side of the room. Give a gourd to the child at the front of each team. At the starting signal, have the first child in each line carry the gourd to a designated spot (such as a numbered chair) on the other side of the room. Then have him return to his team and hand the gourd to the next child in line. Each team finishes when every child on it has carried their gourd across the room and back. Vary the level of difficulty for older students by having them use cups, ladles, tongs, or spoons to carry the gourds.

WALKIN' THE WALK

Hold a Pumpkin Walk to distribute a grab bag of goodies to each party participant. Cut six large pumpkin shapes from construction paper. Write a numeral between 1 and 6 on each pumpkin cutout. Then prepare a grab bag of Halloween goodies, such as candy, pencils, stickers, or tiny toys, for each student. Each bag may contain a different, but similarly appealing, collection of items. Label each bag with a numeral between 1 and 6, using each numeral the same number of times.

When you are ready to begin the Pumpkin Walk, tape the six pumpkin cutouts to the floor. Invite a group of six children to walk around the cutouts as you play Halloween music. Explain that when you stop the music, each child should step onto a pumpkin cutout. Have each child identify the numeral on his pumpkin cutout. Ask him to choose a grab bag bearing that same numeral. Continue with other groups of students until everyone has had a turn and received a prize.

ONE FINAL NOTE

When little ones leave your Halloween celebration, send each of them home with his bag full of treats and a copy of the parent note on page 96. The note outlines important Halloween safety tips. Encourage each child to discuss the note with his family before trick-or-treating on Halloween night.

Haunted-House Pattern
Use with "A Haunted Neighborhood" and "Shadow Puppets" on page 87.

Trick
Hop like a frog.

Trick
Hoot like an owl.

Trick
Clap your hands
five times.

Trick
Make a scary face.

Trick
Make a ghost sound.

Trick
Make a silly face.

Trick
Meow like a cat.

Trick
Stomp your feet.

Trick
Squiggle like a
snake.

Share

Trick
Fly like a bat.

Share

Shadow-Puppet Patterns
Use with "Shadow Puppets" on page 87.

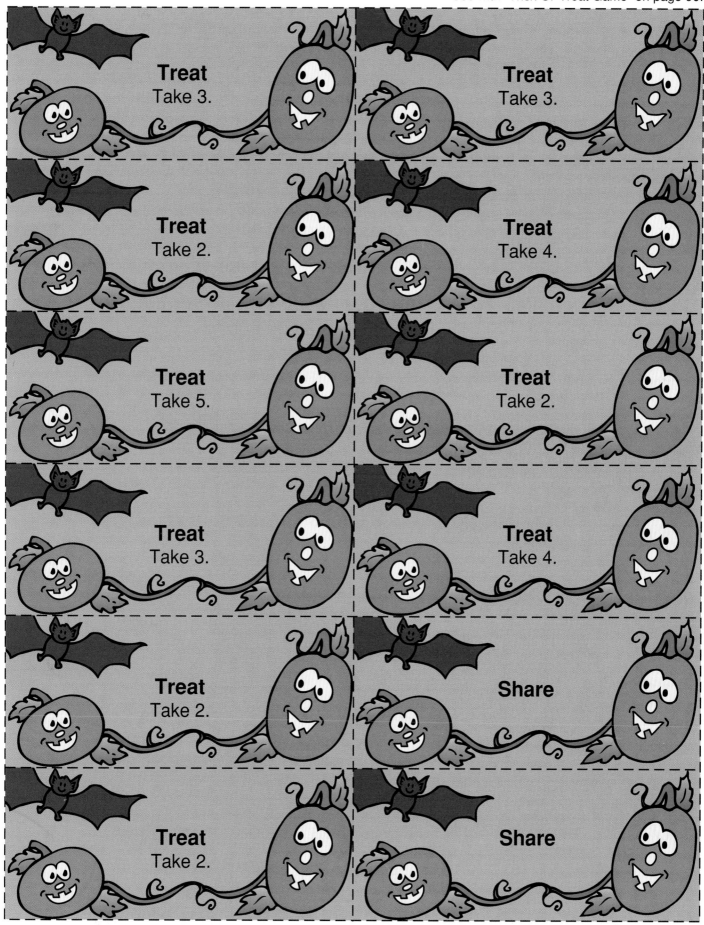

Treat
Take 3.

Treat
Take 3.

Treat
Take 2.

Treat
Take 4.

Treat
Take 5.

Treat
Take 2.

Treat
Take 3.

Treat
Take 4.

Treat
Take 2.

Share

Treat
Take 2.

Share

Dear Family:

It's that time of year again—Halloween! As you and your child prepare for trick-or-treating and other Halloween fun, please remind your child of these important safety tips.

10 TIPS FOR HALLOWEEN SAFETY AND FUN

1. Take an adult along when you go trick-or-treating or to any Halloween parties.

2. If you trick-or-treat from door to door, visit only the homes of friends and neighbors you know.

3. Do not talk to—or take candy from—any strangers.

4. If you trick-or-treat at night, wear some white or reflective clothing, or carry a reflective treat bag. Take a flashlight.

5. If your costume includes a mask, make sure you can see well.

6. Walk on the sidewalk if possible.

7. Watch carefully and hold an adult's hand as you cross the street.

8. Be careful around lighted jack-o'-lanterns.

9. Use good manners when trick-or-treating. Remember to say "thank you."

10. Let an adult check all your treats before you eat them.

Note To The Teacher: Use this reproducible parent note with "One Final Note" on page 91.